A LIGHT ABOVE AND BEYOND

By

XIOMARA MARTINEZ

ISBN-13: 978-0-692-77931-6
ISBN-10: 0-692-77931-0

Printed in the USA

Editor, Deborah A. Grodman

Book photograph and design by Levis Aguila, Lights on Photography

Consulted with Miriam Mendez

Book format by Eli Blyden | www.EliTheBookGuy.com

DEDICATION

I dedicate this book to my best friend, motivator, and the best mother I could have ever wanted, Barbara Maestre. R.I.P. An amazing and complex woman, who stopped living her own life to allow me to live mine. And whose advice and tenderness will stay with me forever.

And to my young daughter Kassandra. I leave this book as a legacy so that she can learn and understand the sacrifice that her grandmother and I went through and faced with courage. I hope that she will find that same courage as she goes through life. More importantly, I hope she understands the wisdom found in this book, so that she can appreciate Life and make a better one of her own.

CONTENTS

PREFACE

Living without a voice is like not living at all. For twenty-eight years, I had no voice. My lips were sealed. My desire to express publicly my personal experience of how domestic violence can affect not only women in general but, more importantly, children, was stymied by my mother.

But after her death I came to realize I needed to speak out, not just a personal need, but as a commitment and an obligation to give hope to others, particularly young adults, whose journey resonates with mine.

I kept thinking about my abusive father. The last time I heard from him was a year before my mom was diagnosed. He had been told that he had pulmonary cancer and had only a few months to live. He realized the end was near and he sent a request, through one of his friend's, to my sister and me. My mom was the one who delivered his message, "Can you tell my daughters I want to see them. I want to ask for forgiveness."

What should I do? I still had no voice, only fear.

We wondered, *"What was his mental state? Was he depressed? As cruel as he had been? Would he be violent again, and knowing that he was dying, seek revenge and try to take my sister's, my mom's, mine, and/or his own life?*

Our collective response was an adamant "No."

My life continued the usual course, but he was always on my mind. As the months passed, someone would tell us he was seen walking down a street in his neighborhood, well enough to get around. I would wonder about him—not quite worry…just wonder about him.

But a year after hearing of my father's illness, my mom was diagnosed with pancreatic cancer. With this revelation, I completely tucked him away, out of my thoughts and focus.

Once my mother passed, my life was placed on hold, indeed, it seemed to cease altogether. My sister and I grieved our loss, and I was especially inconsolable. My strength and purpose to share anything was gone. I was confused, angry, and I lost track of time.

Not long after my mother's death, I found out that my father had died a few months before. I wondered *"How did he die? Was he alone? Did he die alone in a cold hospital or in a warm bed with relatives around? Did he pass quietly or did he suffer?"* And I will always, somewhat selfishly, wonder, *"Did he ever call my name in the last minutes of his life?"*

* * * * *

A few years after my mother passed away, I felt that it was time to do something, to begin to find my voice. Though still grieving my mother's loss, I told myself that she was not going to have died in vain. It came upon me like an explosion that pushed me into a corner and gave me more thrust to share my story. I needed to share our story. I had to share our story. I felt obliged to speak, as a tribute to her, for sacrificing her life for my sisters and mine.

Two images gave me the strength to get out of the black hole of emotion and to tell my story: watching my mother slowly drowning in a pool of pain from my father's abuse; and watching my mother's eyes closing forever as her final words pleaded, "Pray for my girls."

Though I felt I had to tell my story, writing this book was not in my plans. My primary goal was to go around sharing my thoughts and experiences on a larger scale.

Having earned a marketing degree, and become a successful businesswoman, I thought that the message would cover a broader audience much faster through my personal intervention. Talking with audiences, speaking to small groups, and so on. However, my discussing issues of spousal and familial abuse was met with sharp criticism. I was advised that if I publicly spoke about my personal experiences, I would no longer be seen as the success I had been. To the minds of many, it would seem that my life was somehow tainted. And I, unfortunately, allowed this opinion to seal my lips, once again.

But I knew that I had to somehow speak out and after awhile, I began changing strategies. I decided it would be best not to disclose my personal connection as a domestic violence victim but instead speak about my experiences in the third person. To step away from my personal horror story, to mask my own involvement, and speak in broader terms.

To my surprise, I was a total success. To my disappointment, I experienced how a professional woman in a beautiful gown and having achieved some status can be welcomed to speak about the topic in general terms and yet be treated very differently to that of an "ordinary" domestic violence victim or any woman with a "dark-past" who acknowledges that they speak from personal experience. I felt a small sense of shame that, although I spoke about the subject, I could not find the inner courage to identify myself as a victim.

Although my husband and other members of my family encouraged me to speak out, to find my own voice, write a book, I hesitated. "Who would be interested in hearing my story when, unfortunately, there are so many other stories around in the world that are even more painful? Who would care about my mine and my mother's story?"

I had too many questions and concerns after my experience with the critics. I needed to meditate, take my time, listen for the voice of God, and allow Him to guide me before I made such a big decision.

* * * * *

Although I had placed the idea of writing a book aside, it was always on my mind. I may have lost interest, but never hope. Yet sharing my story publicly was not yet in God's plans. My book had to be written at the right time, and this wasn't it. Eventually, God placed all the portents there for me to see and it confirmed that I had to write my story. It would not be easy to have to relive everything again, but I am not a woman who gives up easily. Trying for me is living, and living is learning. If I don't try, I am not doing anything. I flounder. So I finally made up my mind to begin to write my book.

Although I had always felt that public speaking about the subject was the best channel to convey my message, it is interesting how the idea for a book began. As I was sitting in my home office, I found one of my daughter's journals. It was decorated with butterflies and flowers, like any young girl's journal. I opened it to take a peek and I was encouraged by the simple idea that even a child has a story to tell.

And so did I.

I purchased a journal and I began writing my notes longhand, letting the memories flow. Once I started, I realized that I could not stop. Sweet memories came to mind, but more often awful ones. Memories so painful that they made me pause and close the journal. I would go back to it periodically, but it was always a painful experience. I put it away for a while and then, somehow, I lost the journal. But, a year later, while in the process of moving to another house, I found it in a box. I was afraid to open it. I didn't want to open old wounds through my memories. Eventually, I pushed past my fears and opened it. The writing was extremely messy and I had difficulty reading my own writing. But reading what I had written, reading the pain expressed in the words on those pages was a cathartic experience and, through my tears, I realized that I had to continue to write.

Nobody knew that my intentions of writing the book had returned. Since I wasn't even sure whether I was going to finish writing, I thought "Why tell?"

I thought it was going to be an easier process, especially as I was now using a computer. The keyboard seemed more impersonal than writing with a pen. It would allow me some degree of offset from what I was writing; a cold, font appearing on a white screen seemed less frightening than the emotional cursive writing I had reread in my journal. However, when I started writing again, I began feeling the same turmoil I experienced the first time. But it now seemed ten times worse. As my thoughts were being engraved on screen, tears would run uncontrollably down my face as I relived that world of dark memories. I kept writing without looking at the screen, my fingers typing on their own, as though divorced from the words that appeared there. As my story progressed, I found myself facing memories which I had intentionally forgotten. My selective amnesia was fading.

As I went deeper into my memories, I often became physically ill; my hands would shake and my body felt itchy and uncomfortable as if I had ants crawling all over me. There were times when my body temperature would rise as if I was catching a fever. Other times, as I reread what I had written, I would feel "dirty" and have to stop writing to take a shower; hoping to forget my memories, wishing they too could be washed away down the drain.

Sometimes while sitting at my desk I felt it was all useless and ugly and relived the past rejections from those who, though well-meaning, sought to stifle my message. Once again, I thought that this is not how I want people to see me. But that, I realized, was selfish. I told myself to continue writing to inspire others who have also lived with repressed and devastating memories. I reminded myself that my story was meant to encourage others, to help them get past the trauma in their lives, to find the light of faith that I had found. I had been in denial of these memories, but reliving them seemed to make them a little less powerful. I continued on, saying to myself: *"You need to heal, and this book will help you. And not just you, others, too."*

As I continued writing, the words became more fluid, rising like a tide. I drew strength and hope from both my mother's photo, which I always keeps in my office, and from God who is always by my side. As time passed and my writing progressed, I continued seeing more signs that would encourage me to proceed.

As I read what I had written, the words stung as nettles on my heart. Yet, I heard the whisper of God telling me, *"This is me, putting these memories in your mind to write this book. It's not about you, it is about the purpose, to rescue many."* And people who can relate to my struggle understand this message, this unwavering statement: Only God can take us from "ashes to beauty."

As my first draft neared completion, I dealt with an overwhelming dread, and I would awaken in the middle of the night. Should I publish my book? If I do, my past will be revealed. I'll be exposed, and there will be no turning back. What's going to happen with my image? Will people still see me as the same successful businesswoman or will they close doors on me? As I had been told. What about having new business opportunities? Will I lose those prospects? Do I hide in the dark as I have done or dare to share my story? I was restless. Doubt was a demon that haunted my mind.

* * * * *

One Saturday morning, while walking my daily walk routine at the park, meditating and praying to God as I usually do, I noticed a woman about the same age as my mother sitting on one of the benches listening to music on her cell phone. She was the only other person in the park that morning. On one of my turns, around the park, she began lifting her hands while singing a Gospel song, the same song that my mother used to sing. I took a few steps past her, but then stopped. I felt chills and an overwhelming need to go back to her. I had no clue why or what I might say to her. My feelings became stronger the closer I got to her, and as I approached her I felt that God had chosen her to answer my prayer.

I excused myself for interrupting her morning, but told her that I heard her singing one of my mother's favorite gospel songs. She apologized for singing so loudly, and after we exchanged a few pleasantries, she began to tell me her story.

She told me that she was from Cuba and that she was a cosmetologist (as my mother had been). I felt that I was simply to listen and not interrupt, when she added, "I had to leave Cuba because my husband was physically abusing me. I had marks everywhere and I didn't want my son, daughter, and grandkids to see it anymore." She told me that she was praying for all those who suffered as she had suffered, and hoped that they might find solace and guidance. In fact, she said, she wishes there was a book that would inspire those like that.

Right then, I knew. I thanked her for her time and wished her well. I left immediately, and I was astonished and touched that God had answered my prayers that quickly and so directly. I had no more reluctance, my fears had subsided. I would publish my book.

Driving back home, calming thoughts whispered in mind, *"Don't worry about your needs, don't worry about anyone closing doors on you, I will open bigger ones for you! Don't worry about money! I will take care of everything."*

I felt an enormous peace in my heart that is difficult to explain. I knew it was God putting these thoughts and feelings in me. It had become clear to me that God had lead me all the way through the process of writing my book. A book that would tell my story, and, with God's help, help and inspire others. A testimony that God is here, to give everyone hope, especially to those in need.

1 Philippians 4:6-7 KJV, "Be anxious for nothing, but in everything by prayer and supplication, with

thanksgiving, let your requests be made known to God; and the peace of God, which surpasses all understanding, will guard your hearts and minds through Christ Jesus."

– Xiomara Martinez

CHAPTER 1

LIFE IN CUBA

I can still remember the smell of my mother's fresh baked bread filling the air with a comforting aroma that contrasted with the dark, discomforting storm outside, the kind of storm that often occurs in Cuba during the hot, humid summer. I was scared and ran into the kitchen, grabbed the legs of my mother and squeezed them tightly. "It's okay *niña*," she assured me as the winds howled outside. "Everything will be all right."

I looked up and saw her eyes and wide smile, and felt safe. Even though I was only four years old, I realized I had everything I needed—food, a house, and most of all, a loving family. What I didn't realize was, that soon, all of that would change.

Our neighborhood, like most in Cuba, was a misshapen cluster of small houses, with small, shared backyards, and a front door that pretty much opened onto the street. Some, like mine, were lucky enough to have a tiny front yard.

For the most part, everyone got along; you almost had to. You could hear music, smell the cooking, and listen to the arguments coming from the surrounding houses. Everyone knew everyone else—and everyone else's business.

My house was small, just a combined living room, kitchen, and two small bedrooms. My father, mother, and I shared one; my *abuelos* shared the other. Like everyone else, we didn't have much, but it all seemed magical to a four-year-old girl.

My father would get up early every morning, before the neighbor's roosters would crow, so that he could work on his art projects before he went to work. He was a popular underground painter and artist, well known in our town as well as several towns around us. I often heard him say that he wished he was free to just paint and create.

I assumed he was talking about the government, but I would find out later that I was wrong.

Even though it was not considered correct to do so, as the government controlled everything, people still sought him out and he made extra money by selling his paintings and other artistic creations. He could paint as he liked and kept a small "gallery" of works from which to choose. He also received special commissions for paintings, with some commissions coming from officials who should report him for what he was doing! For them, he would carve special frames and placed the paintings under glass. For this, he'd occasionally be given a bottle of the expensive reserved rum; as a special "thank you" to keep the transaction quiet. Since neither party could tell the authorities on the other, mutual bribes like these were the order of business.

I always admired my father's creativity and his care in selecting just the right color and the right amount of detail to make each painting perfect. My father was becoming locally famous and I was very proud of him. On his few days off work, he would sometimes allow me to sit with him while he worked. I would watch him paint while I colored in my coloring book. I liked my crayons—yellow like the bright Cuban sun, green like the palm fronds, purple, like the bruises I saw on my mother's arms.

He would sometimes ask me if the color he chose for his painting was right and I would give him my opinion. He would nod his head and smile at me, "Thank you, *mi corazón*." he'd say, and I'd smile back. He always took so much care of his artwork, and always took such great care of me. He even shared his dream with me.

And they were big dreams. Because he knew so many important people, he planned to get us out of Cuba, to the United States, and there he would be free to paint all the time and he would become a famous—and wealthy—artist. He'd have a large estate, with two houses on it—one for him with his studio and one for me, my sister and grandparents. I could imagine him on television talk shows and visiting his paintings in museums. The way he described everything made it seem so real! It was almost too much for me to take in! I would get so excited I wanted to tell everyone about it. However, all of that was a secret, he would say. I could tell no one about his dream, not even my mother. "We have to live in the real world," he'd remind me. We still had the day-to-day to get through first.

~The Fire~

I loved playing in our little front yard. My dad had paved most of it with concrete so I wouldn't get dirty playing on the dry, dusty ground. He had planted two small palm trees, some jasmine, and gardenia; which always made our front yard smell wonderful. In a shady spot, he had set up a small swing that he had designed just for us. It was just the right size for me and one or two friends to play on; something we loved to do on a hot summer's day.

Some months later, as I was getting ready for bed, I heard my mom yelling for my grandfather and grandmother, Abuelo and Abuela were also yelling and running out of our house. I smelled a smoky odor as my family and neighbors continued shouting. I ran barefoot to see what was happening. As I stepped through the front door, someone grabbed me and held my head to their chest, my face turned toward my house so I couldn't see what was going on. I managed a quick glance as I stepped outside, but all I could see was a forest of legs. It was like it had been when I was lost at the carnival. I couldn't distinguish whose legs I was looking at, or where my parents were in the crowd. I screamed and tried to turn my head, but I was held firm. Over the noise I heard someone calling my dad's nickname, shouting, "Bertico, no! No more! Stop it!" I had no idea what was happening but a terrible notion entered my mind, what if my father was dying? I pushed and pleaded with whoever held me to let me go, but whoever it was held me tight.

I managed to twist my head just a little and saw my father's shoes and pants through the crowd of legs that surrounded him. I also saw my grandfather pushing him away. My father was screaming something and struggling to get up. My mother was there too, her face wet with tears, watching from behind the crowd and several women had their arms around her, comforting her.

Why was my father being pushed away? Why was my grandfather pushing him? Why was my mother hiding behind the people? Why was the air so smoky and smelly? I managed a quick peek as we hurried away and saw several empty water buckets laying in our courtyard while others were thrown in the air, the charred trunks of our palm trees and I heard the faint crackle of the dying embers from within the blackened tree trunk as we ran through our small gate.

My mother held me tighter than the stranger had and as our group walked out into the street, she kept repeating, "It's okay; it's okay. Everything will be all right." From the way she said it, I wasn't certain who she was trying to convince, me or herself.

I had been forbidden to walk over and see our house, and as we walked back now I understood why. One small palm was frond-less, just a burnt black stump and some of the bushes looked like charred weeds. "Did *mi Papi* do this?" I asked my mother as we walked to the front door, but she said nothing. Nonetheless, my father was forced to leave home.

My grandparents tried to make everything as normal as possible for me, but it all seemed strange since my father wasn't there. As we lay in bed, I heard my mother pray and then cry herself to sleep almost every night. I tried to comfort her as best as a four-year-old could. However, when I would ask why she was crying, what had happened, or where *mi Papi* was, she would change the subject or say, "It's okay, now. He's away. He'll come back soon."

Many nights as I slept, I dreamed about my father. My dad always gave me so much love, and I was so proud of him. He often told me that I was the center of his little world. That I was his sun, and he revolved around me. I think that was true because he did so many nice things for me. He always surprised me with an extra gift or two on *Los Reyes Magos* (Three King's Day) even though the Cuban government's policy (*regimen castrista)* was only one gift per child. He always wanted the best for me; tried to teach me table manners, and how to behave like a princess.

He never raised his hand to me or spanked me when I did misbehave, he only gave me timeouts—but that was worse. He would lose his smile and tell me that I had disappointed him, and that hurt me worse than a spanking. I gave him more respect for all the nice things he did for me. Though I loved my mother, if she hollered my name for me to come home when I was a block or so away playing with friends, I'd stay and play for some time more. But when I heard *mi Papi* whistle for me, I dropped everything and ran home.

~Mi Papi~

Besides loving my mother and me, my father loved to smoke and drink. Because he was so popular and had money to buy rum, he often sat on the swing, like a king on his throne, while many of his friends surrounded him until he would get drunk. On a small table to his right were several bottles of rum and our tiny radio. He'd play music and sing loud enough for the neighbors to hear, but no one seemed to complain. I sometimes did, though, because I was trying to sleep and while the loud music was bad enough, the off-key singing of him and his friends was enough to wake the dead. But when I would go out to talk to him, he would promise to keep the music quiet if I would tell him for the hundredth time, *"Tu eres mi heroe; un hombre de billetes no de monedas,"* (You are my hero; you are a man of lots of paper money, not just coins). I didn't know if the saying made much sense, but my saying it to him in front of his friends always made him and his friends laugh. He'd then point to his lips and I would give him a quick kiss, and then he'd nod his head for me to go back into the house. I can still recall the taste of the sweat, cigarette smoke, and rum that mingled on his lips.

* * * * *

Over the next few weeks, I tried to live as normally as I could, but I still missed my father. One afternoon as I was walking home from one of my friend's house with several other friends, I stopped mid-step because I heard something strangely familiar, a low, rambling whistle-like sound. "What happened? Why did you stop?"

"Be quiet and listen," I told them, but the sound had stopped. We waited a minute or so and then walked on. The same thing happened as we walked home the next day, only this time my friends heard it too. They were frightened and ran home, but I stayed to listen. When it started again, I recognized the sound. It was my father's special whistle!

I looked around but couldn't see him. I closed my eyes and just listened to the whistle, turning my head to determine where it was coming from. I opened my eyes and I saw my father step from the shadows of an alley. "*Papi*!" I screamed and ran over and gave him a hug and a kiss. He looked around to see if anyone was looking and took me back into the shadows, bent down, gave me a quick hug and then held me at arm's length to look at me. I looked at him, too. He was thinner, his hair was longer and matted with grease, he had grown a scraggly beard, and he smelled. "I miss you, *Papi*," I said, bending in to hug him, but he held me away. "When are you coming home?" I asked.

"Not for a while, *mi corazón*," he said. "Your grandfather and mother won't let me."

"Why not?"

He thought for a moment, pursed his lips and said, "Because they are mean-especially your mother. She doesn't want me to be with you."

My eyes started to fill with tears. "But *I* want you to come home, *Papi*, I miss you."

"I know, *mi Vida*, and I miss you, too," he said. "But, as long as your mother is so mean, I can't come back. She is too *dura de corazón* (hardhearted).

That didn't sound right to me. My mother cried almost every night, but my father had never lied to me before, so why shouldn't I believe him now? "You're right, *Papi*," I said. "I'm going to tell her to be nicer and let you come back home!"

He smiled, pulled me closer and gave me one last hug, then stood up and said, "Don't say anything to your mother or grandparents. This will be our secret for now. Promise?"

"Okay, but it's not fair!" I said.

He smiled and whispered, "I'll talk to you like this every few days, so listen for my whistle. I love you!" I nodded and he walked away into the alley.

"I love you too," I said as he disappeared into the shadows.

~A liaison~

He kept his promise and I did see him several times. I kept my promise too and said nothing to my mother or grandparents. As I lay in bed trying to sleep, I could sometimes hear them talking about my father, and they would say the most terrible things. After a few weeks of listening to them, I could not bear it any longer and I got out of bed and told them what was going on.

"You are all so mean and I hate all of you!" I hollered at the three of them. "I saw *Papi*, and he told me that you won't let him come back home. Poor *Papi* doesn't have any place to stay or enough to eat. He smells and hasn't taken a shower. He even has a long beard!" No one seemed moved at all by my father's sufferings. "He needs to be here, with us!" I said with all the emotion of a four-year-old girl.

The three of them just stared at me and said nothing for a few seconds, then my mother said, "Xiomara, you always take your father's side and defend him. Sometimes, though, there is no excuse for what he does. You're too little to know what is going on."

"Yes, I do know what's going on," I immediately hollered back. "You hate *Papi*, since I love him, and *you* don't want him back home, that means you hate me too!" I started to cry and ran back to bed. Even then, I knew that it was a hurtful thing to say to my mother. I loved my father, but I loved her too. And maybe, just maybe, I really didn't know what was going on.

No one said anything about my outburst the next morning, and I didn't see my father on the way home from school for a few days after that. When I did, I told him what had happened. He thanked me and told me that I was very brave, and then asked me if I could deliver a message for him.

Over the next several weeks, I was the go-between for him, my mother, and grandfather; carrying messages and replies. Eventually, I took my *abuelo* to meet my father. I could see my grandfather look at him with disgust. My father gave me a quick hug and asked me to step away to let them talk privately. I watched them and could see the tension between them because they didn't shake hands or step closer to each other.

Sometimes they had differences of opinion. But, my grandfather deep inside had a special feeling for my dad, which sometimes would work towards his advantage. And, soon after several meetings like this, they seemed to get along better. I wasn't supposed to hear what they were saying, but I was curious and so pretended not to hear them when I actually did. I heard my father repeat "*lo siento*" (I'm sorry), over and over, promise to stop drinking so much, not to scream at my mother or anyone else in the family, or talk bad about them to anyone. Grandfather told him that the neighbors would also watch out for him and let my grandfather know if he didn't follow the rules. He also said that this would be the last time, and asked him if he understood that.

My father was quiet and nodded, then held out his hand to my grandfather. I watched my grandfather just awkwardly standing at first and then reluctantly take my father's hand and shake it. My grandfather walked toward me, holding out his hand to take mine. My father walked away, waving to me and blowing me a kiss.

~Papi returns~

It was several weeks before my father came back home and before he walked into our house. My mother and grandfather talked with him in the street. *Mi Abuela* kept me in my room while they talked outside. We couldn't hear what was being said, but we could hear their voices get loud several times. I know I heard my father say, *"lo siento"* (I'm sorry) over and over. Finally, my mother opened the door to my room, "Your father's here," she said robotically, showing no emotion.

"Papi!" I shouted and sprang from my bed to greet him. As I did so, I saw my mother and grandmother shaking their heads. Well, that didn't bother me. Even if he had been the cause of the great commotion, I had missed him and was happy to see him.

I told all my friends at school that my father was back home-I was so very happy! But not everyone seemed as happy as I was. My mother and grandparents seemed to only talk to him when they had to, and we often ate our meals in silence. Our neighbors on both sides of us always asked me if everything was all right now that my father was home.

My father tried to be friendly, and when he was home from work, helpful around the house. Even helping to clean the dishes—something he hated to do. I would tell him about my day, what was happening with my friends, and asked him if he needed any help with his paintings, anything to start a conversation. I know that he appreciated that because my mother and grandparents barely spoke to him, but he did talk to me. We'd laugh and share those "daddy and daughter" moments that meant so much. At first, my mother and grandparents were upset by the way he would manipulate me, but eventually, they accepted our relationship, and him, a little more. If we were not a close family now, we were becoming closer than we had been a month or so ago.

I knew that everyone loved *mi Papi* and his art, but that didn't stop people gossiping about him. Did the government know how much extra money he made from his paintings? Were the bottles of rum he bought and shared with his friends a way to keep everyone quiet? How could our family put up with him after what he had done? It was from the gossip that I learned what had happened the night of the commotion.

It wasn't unusual for my father and his friends to be drinking in front of the house, but something seemed to be bothering my father. He had been drinking too much, like always they said. He was talking bad about my mother and grandparents, and how he'd be better off without them, how he could then be a real artist.

The more he drank, the angrier he got, until he became so enraged that he staggered to his paint supplies, retrieved the partially filled bottle that held the kerosene that he used to clean his paintbrushes, and shook some around the front yard, then lit it with his cigar. He started to laugh as the flames grew, no one but him thought it was funny. He knew that my mother was already traumatized by the previous experiences, and he used this tactic to keep her afraid. Since the houses were so close together, a fire was a threat to everyone.

God was always protecting us, and one of my father's cronies drunkenly told my mother that she was lucky because he had been trying to burn the house down, but this time with everyone inside! As I was listening, I then again heard how my grandfather had thrown him out of the house without any success. He begged and begged him for mercy to stay. But those must have been lies. How could *mi Papi* do that? It made no sense to me and I refused to believe it.

My mother allowed my father to sleep with us in the bedroom, and I was so excited to be a family again. I knew as any four-year-old child desires, that things were getting better, and they would stay better. I just knew.

CHAPTER 2

ONCE A LEOPARD

T he Bible says that a leopard cannot change its spots and neither could my father. Jeremiah 13:23 (KJV [King James Version]) "Can the Ethiopian change his skin, or the leopard his spots? Then may ye also do well, that are accustomed to do evil."

Within a few months, he was again drinking heavily and becoming more verbally abusive to the family. He would rant about needing to be free and holler questions like, "Why did we smother him so? He was an artist and should be able to live an artist's life! What did a wife, a kid, and two old people have to do with artistic creativity?"

He would pause and then answer himself, "NOTHING! Except to stifle it!"

My grandfather was usually able to get him to shut up through reasonable discussions. But my mother's way out was to get him even drunker so that he would collapse in a stupor. I remember so clearly a big gathering in the house next to my house. The music was very loud and almost everyone was laughing. But, this was not my mother's case.

She looked afraid and distant. I knew already my mother's expression, just as I knew my father's when he was drunk and about to start an argument. I knew something was about to happen and I just wanted to step away from hurting my mother. I tried the best I could to entertain him as usual. But, this time he crossed the line.

"*Papi*, can you stop drinking?" He would not pay attention, but I would continue to ask, "*Papi*, can you please stop drinking?" My dad was very careless and egocentric in front of his friends.

As he was holding a bottle of beer, he gave me another one and told me, "I know you are as strong as I am! You are my hero Xiomara! You are my masterpiece!"

As I looked at him smiling, and to avoid more arguments, I took the beer that he had given me and drank it all. He was laughing with joy when he realized that I was indeed his masterpiece, I was just four years old. I could hardly walk and saying words that made no sense.

As I was heading to sit under a big tree that my friends and I used as a hideaway, one of my mom's friends saw me walking in that direction and rushed to get my mom. But, I was already on the floor almost unconscious. My mother was furious. I could only hear neighbors rushing and screaming for ice. I was falling asleep, but the neighbors were trying to keep me awake throwing ice all over my body.

* * * * *

We all knew what to expect. The next morning my father would apologize and beg everyone's forgiveness. For a few days, he'd behave himself and then one of his friends would stop by, the rum would flow and he'd show his spots again. This became a weekend occurrence.

His drinking became so bad, just as my mother's fear for him. For some reason, my mother forbade him to return to her bed and made me share the bed with him every night. I felt bad for him and kept him from being lonely.

Still, I could sense that things were getting worse, and I knew it, even if I wouldn't acknowledge it. Even at five years old, I sensed a doubt about my family life. But, I had always been resilient, and I eventually just got used to an increasingly alcoholic, abusive father. As it would happen, he and I seemed to draw closer because of our failings.

You see, the stress of living like that caused me to become a bed-wetter. Because this was so sudden, my mother asked our neighbors advice on how to prevent these scenarios and how to protect the bed from my wetting. Now, everyone knew about my problem, which only embarrassed me and made matters worse. My mother would have to launder the extra thick blanket she had put on my side of the bed to absorb my urine every day, and it was upsetting to help her put it on the clothesline in our backyard for all the neighbors to see.

I was ruining the mattress in our house, and it seemed I could not control myself no matter what I did, or what the neighbors suggested to my mother. I had so much guilt that I could not face my mom, grandparents, or even my dad. Just knowing that she had to wake up sometimes in the middle of the night to a damp, smelly mattress, and awaken me to pat it dry was devastating.

My mother would put a few drops of cheap cologne on it to help hide the smell before we'd drag it to the backyard and let the bright sun dry the mattress and bleach the stain.

I was not getting better over time, and even though I continued to wet the bed, he never complained. I now think that it was an unspoken agreement that if I put up with the smell of his alcohol, he'd put up with a damp mattress. Maybe, because I sensed the difficulty we had facing our problems, there was a grudging mutual respect; and I eventually overcome mine and slept soundly and drily, though the night.

I tried to live as normal a life as possible—playing with my doll, playing games with my school friends, and trying to block out what I knew—or thought I knew—about what was happening in my family. I often heard my mother and father in whispered argument, and I would hide to try to listen to their conversations. I knew that I would become anxious and end up worried, but I couldn't help myself. I just had to know what was going on.

~Your Father Is No Saint~

He was gone again. Once more I had no father. No one to love me like he did, to inspire me, or to be my best friend. If he made a few mistakes, why couldn't my mother forgive him? After all, she had done it before. My father was just like me in looks and temperament, so if my mother couldn't love him—did that mean that she couldn't love me?

I really never gave myself a chance to find out, because I became a brat, from almost the moment my father left. I defied my mother at every turn, didn't do my chores around the house, or did them poorly so that my mother would have to redo them. I would neglect my homework, and my mother would be called to the school. I was simply miserable for my mother and grandparents to put up with. I would never listen to them and always try to get my way. When she would holler at me or spank me, I always screamed at her, "You're not my boss! *Mi Papi* is my boss!", and I would run to a corner in the bedroom and cry out my anger. I never realized how much I was hurting her.

At one point, my mother had had enough of my childishness and took me into the bedroom, made me sit on the bed, and started to talk. I had never seen her so angry and I became a little afraid. She stood by the bed, towering over me and sternly said, "Xiomara, I told you before that you were too little to understand what's going on, but you made it your business to find out. You think you know everything, but you don't. And I can tell you that half of what you think you know is wrong." She sat on the bed beside me and continued. "You have to understand that your father is not the great man you think he is. He is a drunkard. He broke his word to me and to God, and I cannot forgive him anymore."

I immediately became angry and started to defend my father, but before I could finish the first few words, my mother raised her voice and said, "It is time you shut up and listen to *me!*" I sat back, startled. "Your father is no saint—far from it. Truly, he isn't even much of a man." She paused for a moment and looked at me. "I never wanted to have to tell you this, but your attitude has pushed me where I never wanted to go. I'm mad at you for that!" Again, she was silent, then took a deep breath, sighed and said, "Your 'perfect *Papi*' never wanted you in the first place. He wanted me to have an abortion, and if I hadn't heard the voice of God as I lay on that clinic table, you wouldn't be here now."

I knew what an abortion was because one of my mom's friend had one, I once heard. I couldn't believe that my father would have told my mother to get one. I could feel my face flush and my lips turn into a pout. He never wanted me! So why did he pretend to love me? My mother slid closer and put her arm around me. "I know you think he loves you," she said, lowering her voice to console me. "And he does in his own way, but it's not the right kind of love." I looked up at her thinking that if love is love, how can it be wrong?

"Your father used me and you. He spent time with us only when he chose to and only because he had to." I scrunched up my face and stared at my mother. That just didn't seem possible to me. "He wasn't always that way, Xiomara. You can ask your *abuelos* about the man he was. I don't know what changed him but whatever it was, living with him became a misery. And once he started getting some extra money and drinking, things only got worse."

"We tried to hide it from you as best we could, but it became harder and harder. Sometimes, I'd have to ask for food from our neighbors because your father spent his extra money on rum, for him and his friends. Do you remember how your father used to get drunk and would holler at your *abuelos*, and scream at me? You would get so scared that you'd run to us and beg us to stop fighting? Do you remember that?" I nodded my head. I did remember.

"The neighbors were so afraid for us that they had to come over to make sure we were okay, and then take your father away to sleep off his drunkenness." She paused and wiped the tears from her eyes. "And when he would get so fed up with us, he'd just leave; just walk out and be gone for days. I always told you that he was painting in another neighborhood, but I had no idea where he went." Her voice trailed off and my mother grew quiet for a moment. She then looked at me, took my head in her hands and kissed me on the forehead. "The only reason I ever let him come back...was you." I could feel my eyes grow wide.

"I couldn't stand to see you so upset when he was gone or fail to see how happy you were when he was here. I knew that he was poison to me, but he seemed like a tonic for you." It was true that I always felt better when my father was with us. He always made me happy and cared for me. Yet, just as I began remembering all the wonderful times I had with my father, a question popped into my mind. "*Mimi*," I asked, "if *Papi* loved me so much, why did he try and burn our house down? I was in the house, *Mimi*. Why would he do that?" My mother put her arm around me and pulled me closer to her. She shook her head and said, "I don't know, *mi Vida*. I just don't know."

We sat silently for a moment and then she said, "I should have alerted the police; but again, he has too many connections in town, it is useless and I thought of losing you. Your *abuelos* thought I was foolish—and I think they still do—but I gave him another chance for your sake. But now he's run out of chances. No more, *mi Vida,* no more." She looked down at me and asked, "Do you understand things a little better now?" I looked up at her and shook my head.

Things did make more sense now. Things made sense, but I was yet too young to capture many of the details. I did know that I still missed *mi Papi,* but I also knew that I understood my mother and how desperate she feared to lose me through his manipulation.

~My Secret~

It was some time later but just as before, my father seemed to become sober and approached my grandfather about coming home. My mother refused, "For now; maybe someday" she'd say, but she did allow my father to see me, but only if he had not been drinking and there was someone else there.

Since I understood how hurtful he had been, it was hard for me to deeply love him, as I had before. Still, he was my father and he had always made the effort to be kind to me. It was awkward at first, not just seeing him, but having a chaperone with us. Over time, though, we found that we could build a small bridge between us.

He still had his dream, he said and spoke loud enough for my *abuelo* to hear, that maybe, just maybe, we'd all be leaving Cuba. *"Secreto,"* he whispered, putting his finger to his lips. "You must keep it a secret, Xiomara. Can you do that?"

"Si, Papi!" I shouted, then looked around and lowered my voice, "Sorry, *Papi*. Yes, I can keep our secret!" He smiled and nodded, kissed my forehead, and left. I could hardly sleep for the next few nights; my imagination was on fire.

As the months passed, my dream of my father's dream coming true faded away, until the colorful imaginings became nothing more than a muddled mass of grays and blacks. His visits became less frequent, but when I would see him, I'd always ask him about it and my father would just tell me that, "These things take time" and I was to trust him. For me, with all that I knew, trust was something rationed, like the food at the *Mercado*. I barely had enough trust for my mother and grandparents, and I wasn't certain that I could afford some for him.

Not only were my father's visits with me becoming less frequent but so was the money he had promised to give my mother. As the 1980s began, the Cuban economy worsened and there was growing unrest within the country. I remember listening to the radio one day when the announcer said, that almost ten-thousand people tried to gain asylum at the United States embassy. My mother explained, "asylum" meant safety from abuse, and that is when I knew what I wanted for my family—asylum.

It was easy for me to understand why, for even in our little town there were constant shortages of rice, beans, and other staples. Meat was a scarce item, and people guarded their chickens jealously; because thieves stole them if they weren't carefully watched. The government didn't know how to handle the increasing number of people dissatisfied with their lives, and they worried about an uprising. Finally, it was decided that it was better to let these "malcontents" to leave, and they allowed screened mass departures from Mariel Harbor.

The harbor was around forty-five kilometers from our town, and the radio and television talked about how crowded it already was. The government was controlling who could get out and had set up secured gates and barbed wire fencing around sections of the port to keep control. The television's fuzzy black and white images of crowds outside the gates and fences, waving to those inside, were as chaotic as the masses of people on the screen. The radio commentary wasn't much clearer.

All we knew for certain was that those who were leaving were "*gusanos*" (worms). Who had turned their backs on the revolution and their "fellow Cubans". They were enemies at worst, and objects of derision at best.

When I came home from playing with my friends, I saw my grandfather and mother sitting at our small kitchen table, he was holding her hands and she was crying. I rushed to her, "What's wrong, *Mimi*," I asked. She just reached over and hugged me. My grandfather shook his head and mumbled something. All I could make out was my father's name and the word *gusano*. My eyes widened and I understood what was happening.

I broke free of my mother's embrace and ran down the street looking for my father. I checked the bars, his friend's houses, even our church, but couldn't find him. I was about to run home when I realized there was one place I hadn't looked, the most obvious place I should have looked, the bus station.

The bus station was small and overly crowded as I fought my way through the throng of people. The few police that were available tried to keep everything under control, but it was very hectic. People stood in lines holding money in one hand and small suitcases in the other; with old sheets rolled up as makeshift carriers slung across their backs that held the rest of their possessions. They were shoving each other to get close to the ticket window, and everyone was shouting for a ticket to the same destination, "Mariel."

I turned left and right and pushed every which way, but didn't see mi *Papi*. "Have you seen my father?" I asked. "Have you seen, Bertico?" No one paid any attention to me and several were so annoyed at me that I was pushed out of their way. I found myself being shoved away from the window towards the bus stop and the already crowded bus.

Even though it was outside, the area stank of diesel exhaust from the bus, as it started its motor, preparing to depart. A policeman hollered over the noise of the people and the motor and asked me what I was doing, but before I could ask him about my father, he stepped away to stop a fight that had started in one of the lines. I looked up at the bus, with its mud-caked tires and dirty windows and saw fleeting silhouettes of faces as the sun began to set. *"Maybe he's already on the bus?"* I thought and stepped closer to look for my father. I jumped as high as I could to get a better look inside, but it was hard to see. *"Maybe he's on the other side?"* I thought and ran to the other side of the bus to look there. *"Papi?!"* I yelled as loudly as I could. But, my father was nowhere to be found.

My mother, out of desperation, finally told me the truth. "Your dad left to go to the United States."

"He would never leave without giving me a kiss," I replied. *"Papi, Papi,* where are you?" My mother felt guilty for not telling me the truth, I rushed to where he was, The Harbor. I was able to make it and see him from far away. It *was* my father! A fence between us was keeping us apart. I could not even reach out and touch his hands to say goodbye.

"*Papi, Papi,* why are you going to leave me? I promise you that I will never wet in the bed. Don't leave me!"

"I'll be back for you!" He continued to tell me desperately. I could see his tears glistening in the light of the setting sun.

"But when?" I asked. "Can't I come with you, now? When, are you coming back for me?" Before he could answer me, an arm reached over and pulled me away.

"You shouldn't be here, *niña*," the policeman said, as he yanked me to the side, I heard the sounds of a horn and watched the bus pull away.

I broke free, as I could still see hands waving out of a window and imagining that one of them was my father's, bidding me goodbye. I walked back through the crowds and realized that something big was happening. My father wouldn't be coming back. And, in fact, he never did.

CHAPTER 3

A CHANGE
IS COMING

Through the years, I blamed my mother for allowing my father to leave and not tell me. I was used to their behavior. He was in and out of the house, but at the end of the day, he was always around. This time it was different, my dad was gone. Every morning, I would sit outside on the porch waiting for a "sign." Hoping and praying that everything was just a dream and that I would awake and everything would be as he discussed. I would wonder, maybe he missed the bus or changed his mind. I would listen for his whistle or the sound of his voice. But there was never any signs of him.

I asked my mother, "Mimi do you think he is going to call me?"

"I'm sure he will call you Xiomara." But I knew it was said for my sake and not because she believed it.

Over time I started to lose trust in my mother and came to believe that she was never telling me the truth. I became very rebellious towards her, wouldn't do my chores, be late for school, and would do anything to make her upset. It was a young daughters misunderstanding of what I would later understand to be her protection of my feelings.

Then one day, I heard my mother calling me from several blocks away, "Xiomara, your dad is on the phone!" I ran as fast as I could, thinking that I would see him. But it was only his voice on the phone. Looking back, I don't know what hurt most, having seen him leave on the bus, or only being able to hear his voice without having him there to hug. I was so young and these feelings were so unfamiliar to me.

"Xiomara," he said, "I'm in the *Estados Unidos* (the United States). I want you to know that I will come back for all of you. You don't have to worry, Xiomara, I promise I will call you every day, around five o'clock."

The U.S. was not too many miles away, but far enough for me to understand how empty and lost I was going to be without him. But hearing from him every day made me happy.

"I understand *Papi*," I said. I ran over to my mom and hugged her. "Mimi, *Papi* is going to be calling me every day, at five o'clock, please make sure I don't miss his phone call."

But I didn't have to worry about her missing the phone call, as every day at 5:00 p.m., I was sitting by the telephone waiting for his call. Hearing his voice was the only thing I looked forward to each day. I felt even closer to him every time I held on to a doll that he had sent to me. Together my doll and I never missed a phone call.

Meanwhile, my mother did everything she could to fill the void left by my dad and tried to mend our relationship. But, it never happened.

"Mimi, *Papi* didn't call today," I yelled at my mother. "He told me every day he would call at 5:00 p.m., and now it is already 7:00 p.m.!" My dad had been calling me every day for the first few weeks and then the phone calls started to decline as time passed. But my mother promised me that he was certain to call the next day. Or the next day. Or the one after that.

She didn't answer me. I saw her walk away with two friends, whispering. I sensed that something was not right.

"You promised me that he would call me every day Mimi!"

"No Xiomara, *I* told you I was sure he would call you. Your dad loves you very much, but phone calls from the United States to Cuba are very expensive. He needs to save money so he can come back for us."

I understood but was disappointed. Was it the truth? And if not, who was lying to me—my mother or my father?

* * * * *

I tried to get back to my normal life and concentrated on going to school and playing with my friends. Knowing the words "coming back for us" was sufficient, enough for me to be happy.

With time, I found someone that I thought could fill my dad's space, my *Abuelo* (grandfather). However, my *Abuelo* was not child-oriented, and I wasn't even sure if he really liked my company. After all, I had defended my dad all those times, when he knew my mother was suffering from my dad's abuse. Not just that, it seemed that we basically had nothing in common.

However, a few weeks later I asked, "*Abuelo*, can I play with you? I can be the teacher and you can be my student." He was a man of few words. In fact, he hardly spoke to anyone. I was surprised when he replied, "Yes." I was surprised and happily so. This gesture totally opened my eyes.

We began to play together, to talk with each other and before too long, my grandfather had taken on my father's role. It was such a beautiful feeling to have a father-figure. I looked forward to him picking me up at the end of my school day and having a companion to walk home with.

As we walked to his home one day he said, "Sit here with me. Do you want *arina* [cornmeal], your *abuela* made some?" It was his favorite plate and his tradition to have it every day. "Yes, *Abuelo*!" I answered.

My grandfather would never sit in the main dining room to eat his meals. He preferred his bedroom and it was there, at a small table, where he would eat alone. Except when he ate *arina* with me.

It felt magical—each day I would sit face to face with him eating *arina*; and though he never spoke during the meal, just looking at him and being with him was enough for me. After we ate, I would then tell him that I was going to do homework and then play with friends. I would kiss him on the cheek and he would crack the barest of smiles—it really made his day. Little by little, *Abuelo* and I became inseparable.

A few weeks later I told my mother, "Now I have someone to listen and respect. You are not the boss of me anymore because now it is *Abuelo*."

I said it with a sense of pride, happy to have him in my life. But I didn't realize that what I was saying would hurt her so. Yet, it felt good to me to finally be able to have a father-figure again. I was still angry with her, still blaming her for my father's absence. I was just so angry that I didn't realize how much she loved me and how much my words had hurt her.

Days and months passed. My mother reluctantly came to understand my new relationship with my grandfather and accept if, if not approve of it. Indeed, my grandfather and I grew closer every day. I watched as he transformed from being a solitary, lonely man to my loving *Abuelo*. And it was't about *arina* anymore, it was more mature than that. Now it was about having Cuban coffee and cookies. "Xiomara, it is time for our coffee," he would say, and I would run towards the small magical table.

By then, we were having conversations. His calm voice and attention to what I had to say made my love and appreciation for him grow. We talked about all sorts of things. Well, as many things as would interest a nine-year-old girl and her grandfather.

As a typical nine-year old, I wanted to stay with my friends, my grandmother, and mostly my grandfather. I had forgotten about my father's promise to bring us to the United States. But the time to leave was approaching.

My mom had to find a creative way to guide me away from my *Abuelo* without my knowledge. She started discussing the possibility of us going to the United States. Several times a day she would ask, "Don't you want to go to the US and see your dad?"

I did. But what about my grandfather? "I'm not leaving *Abuelo* behind," I protested. He is very old, and who is he going to eat with him and entertain him after we leave? And I don't want to leave my friends, Mimi." And then I said some of the most hurtful words of all, "Why again, Mimi? Why do you have to take everything away from me every time?"

"What am I going to do with Xiomara?" I overheard her asking a friend. "First she loses her father and now her grandfather. But this is what we had planned. It's for her own good and for a much better future. She is going to have to do what I say. There is nothing else to discuss."

~The bloody Streets~

The neighborhood dogs and strays were constantly barking for several nights. The noise was loud enough to keep people in my neighborhood awake and enough to make me feel certain that something horrible was going to happen. I had been told that when a dog barks so desperately it is usually a sign of warning that something or someone is sneaking around. "When they bark with such persistence, they're intention is to protect us from dangerous situations," I would hear adults saying.

"Mimi," I asked my mom, bleary-eyed from lack of sleep, "are we in danger? The dogs won't stop barking."

"Everything is ok, mi *niña*, go back to sleep," she replied reassuringly. "Okay," I said, and went back to bed.

During the day, however, I would see her looking around suspiciously and whispering with friends. Was someone in danger? Was it us? My mother had been in danger before and I could not stop thinking the possibility that it might be her.

Every night it was the same. Nothing could stop the dogs from barking. Flashlights in hand, all the neighbors searched the streets and backyards. My experience of seeing those lights in the dark was scary enough for me to hide in a closet for safety. Sometimes my friends and I would be together in one persons house while the adults searched the neighborhood. Thankfully, during those several nights, nothing was found. And at sunrise we kids would come out of wherever we were hiding and our daily routine would start all over.

Though I was a child, I realized that something was not right. I told my mom, "Mimi, I'm afraid that someone might be underneath my bed".

She smiled. "What makes you believe that Xiomara?" I didn't have an answer. I think she thought that I was simply worried rather than that maybe I had seen something strange in our neighborhood. But, truth be told, it was one of the first times I had a sense of intuition—a foretaste of something yet to come. Something I would experience throughout my life.

After a few nights, it fell silent. There were no dogs barking, no flashlights in the night, no neighbors prowling the streets. People slept quietly, and everything seemed back to normal. Everything except my intuition.

"Why do I have flashbacks of *Papi* hurting you, Mimi? Why, am I so worried for you if *Papi* is so far away?" I asked my mother. She tried to comfort me, but I could not shake the feeling that something was amiss. The mysterious barking of the past few nights, the unknown and unseen, and now the overwhelming silence was making me think even more of the past.

"My dad is 90 miles away. I need to let go of unpleasant thoughts. We are safe," I tried to force myself to believe. "Mimi, I don't hear the dogs tonight, so why am I worried?" "Don't be," she said softly. "It's quiet and it's late. We can all finally rest." I started to say something, but as I was talking to her, I fell asleep.

Then, suddenly, the dogs begin to bark louder than they had before. The same commotion that I had experienced in my early childhood started over again. I got out of bed and looked out the window. People were screaming and running in toward one of our neighbors homes. I went to get my mother.

"Mimi, where are you?" I looked about but couldn't find her. She wasn't in the house, so I ran out and asked a neighbor if they had seen her. "Stay here," she said, and grabbed her daughter. "You two stay here," she said and ran off with the crowd. We grasped each other's hands, frightened and wondering what was going on.

We heard shouting from three houses down the street."*La mato! La mato!"* (He killed her! He killed her!) My friend and I held each other more tightly realizing that the house was that of one of our friends. A woman we both knew had been stabbed.

While my best friend and I were holding on to each other, we heard someone scream, *"Se le estan saliendo los intestinos,"*—"Her intestines are coming out!" It was impossible for us not to panic—and that is exactly what we did. We held each other closer, our bodies trembling with fear and wondered what to do. But curiosity got the better of both of us and my best friend and I went up that narrow, dark road right above our house level to get a better glimpse of the situation, but still holding hands as we walked.

We could barely see what was happening as it seemed that the entire neighborhood was surrounding her. Women and men knelt around her, and I found out later that the woman holding her hand, offering what comfort she could, was my mother!

We did see people trying to stop the woman from bleeding to death using pieces of their own clothing to staunch the flow of blood. It was a gruesome sight for children to see.

"Hey," someone shouted, "where did he go?" The crowd began to separate, flashlights waving light beams in the dark as they looked about for the murderer.

Once he had been discovered, and he heard the shout, *"La mato, La mato."* he ran away down the street. But, just where had he gone?

Our curiosity soon became our nightmare. My friend and I saw something lying in the middle of the street. It was dark where we were standing and though we could hardly see, it looked it was a body and we approached it, cautiously, to get a better look.

It was a man, on his knees, holding something shiny in his hand. My friend and I looked at each other. Did he hear us approaching? Would he rise up and chase after us?

We stopped where we were, coming no closer, and both of us trembled as we watched him slightly tilt his head up and the shiny object swipe across his throat. At first, a small amount of blood was slowly coming out from his neck. Then a flow of blood sprayed high into the air like a water fountain. His body buckled and he fell onto the street. Blood began to flow everywhere. We were too terrified even to look away. We watched his body convulse and shake. We suddenly found our courage and we began to scream, *"He is here, He is here."* Someone heard us and shouted, *"Over There!"* and we could see flashlight beams coming our way.

My friend and I had watched our friend's mother as she lay almost dying in the dusty street, and now had watched her father commit suicide. Several men were now with us and I suddenly I felt like I was flying, like a butterfly, as someone picked me up and carried me away from my friend and that horrible scene.

I couldn't sleep that night, or for the next several nights. It had all been too ghastly for a child to see.

My friend's mother miraculously survived, but she would never be the same.

My heart went out to my friend who had lost her father and almost her mother, too. And though I suffered from nightmares about what I had seen, I needed to know more.

I asked my mother what had happened but she refused to tell me, even about her part in helping the poor woman, so I listened to the gossip over the next few days and discovered what transpired that night.

For several days, my friend's father had been watching her mother for a few nights, hiding among the bushes in the small alley to spy on her. That was the reason why the dogs were barking.

He had warned her days before that he was going to kill her, even telling some of their neighbors, but nobody thought that he would actually do it. After all, they said, every family fights but *"Perro que ladra no muerde"*—a dog that barks, doesn't bite—was my friend's mother's reply. And always with a smile on her face, she would add, "He doesn't have courage enough to do it." She was wrong. Dead wrong.

Those who had tried to save her said that the front of her body was covered with holes in the shape of the knife blade. But, the final wound was impossible to forget. For him, it was his grand finale, as he yelled at her, loud enough for the neighbors awakened and running to the house to overhear, *"This is for you!"* he stabbed her mouth by inserting the knife from the top right of her lips to the bottom of the left side. He screamed, *"Yes, a dog that barks can bite."*

Jealousy. That had been the cause. Insinuation led to arguments that led to verbal, and then, physical abuse. Domestic violence sputtered out of control and led to attempted murder and suicide.

"Now what?" I wondered. The front doors in our neighborhoods are usually left open for anyone to enter. Sure, we closed them at night to keep the insects and strays out of the house, but few ever locked their doors. Until now.

I had suffered from my parents' domestic abuse in so many cases but I had blocked a lot of it from memory. When I begin to comprehend what it was all about, the fear of my mom being killed and thinking that *my father* could kill my mom the same way was definitely in my mind. I was horrified by the thought that I might see my mother's body stabbed like that or my dad's throat cut.

I looked up towards where we had found the body, and there were still people brushing off the blood from the street. What had seemed a nightmare was all too true.

It took several months for me and my friends to cross that street without fear. In fact, the word fear did not fit any longer, the word 'petrifying' was more apt, for when we approached the spot, we paused, rock-still, in horror. Indeed, both streets that we had played on as children became the streets of horror.

For me, it felt as if I was playing baseball. Staying on base, watching around and moving to the next base only if I saw it was safe. That became my everyday behavior, especially at night. If I was out when it was dark I would count, one, two, three…go, running from point to point.

And every time I heard a dog bark at night, I could feel my forehead dampen with the cold sweat of panic.

And worse, I began bedwetting again. Now I realize the cause, but at the time, it was embarrassing. The shock and damage to my awareness would cause me to occasionally wet the bed until I was eleven years old, and finally better able to cope with what I had experienced.

If anything good came from all of this, it was that I began to recognize my mother as a hero, not just to her friend, but to me as well.

CHAPTER 4

THE INEVITABLE

y mother and father used to wake me up in
the middle of the night and surprise me with
a short trip to the beach. I loved the fact that
it was not planned and it was a surprise. But, I learned,
surprises are not always good.

One night, when I was about 11 years old, my mom
did the same thing. She woke me up in the middle of the
night. "Xiomara," she whispered, "let's go."

"Where? Are we going to the beach?" I asked. I was
so excited! I quickly dressed, and looked about for my
swimsuit. But something was very different. Something
felt very odd.

It was so very dark, and a single light illuminated the street. There was a white van in front of our house, and our neighbors and friends had gathered and were whispering, crying and hugging my mom. Then, everything started happening fast. I had the same uneasy feeling when my dad had attempted to burn down the house.

Using hand signals and whispers, they hurriedly placed me in the van. My small suitcase had been packed and was already there. I asked my mother what was happening, but she just squeezed may hand, and said nothing. As we drove away, all I could see from a small hole in the back of the van were our neighbors and friends waving goodbye. Where was my *abuelo* and *abuela*?

~A trip with no return~

After some time, we arrived at a small airport. I was confused. An airplane? First, it was the van and now an airplane?

I'm not sure whose hands were shaking more- me or my moms. There were no friends or family around to guide us. But my mom seemed to know what to do. As we walked from the small terminal to the stairs that led to the plane, my mom looked back toward the building and then the surrounding countryside and could not stop crying.

It was so painful to see. It made me think back to the times when my dad physically abused her. I begged my mom for us not to get on the plane. But she forced a smile, took my hand, and we walked up the stairs.

"Are we going somewhere far?" I asked, once we were seated. But she refused to say. I had never been on an airplane before, and I was a little afraid of this big, mechanical bird. In addition, I was still confused about what was happening. But though I was both anxious and excited, once we took off and was in the air, I began to relax a little and soon the drone of the engines put me to sleep.

I awoke to a small bump that shook the airplane, just as the engines roared louder and then subsided. We were on the ground. I looked up at my mother and asked her what was happening. She turned to me and said, "Xiomara, we are in another country now. We are in Panama."

"*Panama?*" I thought to myself. "*Why Panama? Are we gusanos now?*"

"We'll stay here for several days… and we will soon be meeting your dad in the United States."

What? So many questions! So many emotions! I was confused, sad at missing my *abuelo* and friends, and scared at what meeting my father would be like.

A car picked us up at the airport. Driving through the streets of Panama was amazing! It truly felt like another world from my small town in Cuba. I looked out the car window and took it all in. Crowds of people were out shopping. There were all types of stores: for clothing, for food, a video store a pharmacy, and gas stations everywhere! The busses we passed played music inside for their passengers. Everything looked so big; it was very overwhelming.

The car dropped us off in front of a church. *"What are we doing at a church?"* I wondered. Back in Cuba, we had a church, very close to our house, and we attended regularly. But why stop here at this one?

We stood with our little suitcases on the sidewalk and a woman approached us from the church. My mother spoke with her and asked for the priest by name. The woman nodded, and walked back into the church. I knew that we were not here for a visit or to say a prayer.

When the priest came out, my mother introduced herself and handed him a letter.

"What is that letter for Mimi?" I whispered to her.

"Hush, Xiomara, don't say a word now. Just let him read the letter. He is the one that is going to help us here." This was a letter of recommendation from the priest back in our town. The letter asked him to take care of us for a few days.

I looked at her and trusted her word. The priest returned the letter to her, walked with her a few steps, talking with her as he did so, and then walked back into the church.

My mother held out her hand to me and she led me one of the benches nearby. She sat down slowly and started to cry. She looked devastated. I felt my heart breaking and started to cry myself as I watched her losing control.

"Please don't cry, Mimi. Our Lady of Charity (*Nuestra Virgencita De La Caridad Del Cobre*) promised me that she will take care of us. I have faith. I'm sure that she is here with us." But it didn't matter. My mother explained that the priest was unable to help us. That the reality of the situation was that we were alone in a country where we had never been, had limited funds, and were homeless. We hugged each other and cried. But I believe in God. I believe in Angels. And deep within me, I knew that everything was going to work out.

It was almost dark, the streetlights were coming on, and the church portico was lit in an incandescent glow. People had walked past us all day, but now there were but a few. Perhaps this bench would be our room for the night, until we could think what to do. Then a woman passing by stopped when she saw my mother crying and asked her what was wrong.

My mother explained that we just got off a plane from Cuba that morning, we had no place to stay and the priest that was supposed to help us just said that he was not able to. The woman listened to our story and then did something remarkable. Not only did she take us to her house for a few days, until my dad sent money, but she found us a room to rent right across from her house, while we waited for my dad to send someone for us. It turned out that this lady was also a Cuban refugee who spent 20 years in Panama.As a child, and even today, I think that the lady was an angel sent from God to protect us. What better testament to the love of God and His promise to look over us.

We settled in for our short stay. The cramped room we rented consisted of three small folding beds, a small table with two chairs, a small window, with the only light at night coming from a single bulb on the ceiling. However, days became weeks and the weeks became months. My dad lacked the funds to get us out of the country.

My mother became a virtual slave to the homeowner—cooking and cleaning the house. Since we had no legal documentation, we could only spend time in the room or visit the church. We stayed there a total of eleven months.

* * * * *

I was 12 years old and although I was re-establishing communication with my dad, it didn't feel the same. The *Papi* of memory was being replaced by the dad of reality. Even though he called every evening, it didn't really matter. Too much had transpired. I had witnessed my mother's strength and courage, and realized exactly how much she had sacrificed for me—and how unknowing and ungrateful I had been. My mom was now the center of my life. She had risked all, believing in my father's and the priest's promise, only to be disappointed. Still, she persevered. Still she had faith; faith that everything would work out. Faith that, with hope fading and alone in a foreign country, God would watch over us. A faith I felt also, and clung to.

~A sad farewell~

For my mom, maintaining communication with my grandparents in Cuba gave her the strength to move on. One day the phone rang at an unusual time.

"Barbara, you have a call from Cuba," said the owner of the house. My mother thanked her and picked up the receiver. "*Hola?*" she said. And within seconds my mom started screaming, crying, and almost fainted. She became hysterical. The receiver almost fell from her hand. My beloved *abuelo* had passed.

"It was my fault; it was all my fault! I should have been there and I wasn't! I left him alone," she cried.

I didn't know what to do, or say, or how to react. I too was hurt and devastated, but I had to be strong and give her the support she needed. I held her and repeated over-and-over, "Please don't cry Mimi, please don't cry."

"Here's what happened…" my *abuela* said. But knowing how she would react, my grandmother didn't want to tell my mother the truth about my grandfather death. She just told her he died of heart failure and that he did not suffer. She told her not to feel guilty for leaving, as it was best for me to get an education I would never be able to have one in Cuba. My mother asked her how my grandfather had taken the news of our departure. "He took the news very calmly. You know how he is," said my grandmother.

However, truth always prevails, and years later my mom found out what actually occurred. The morning following our departure from Cuba, my grandfather looked for us and asked her where we were. My grandmother told him that we went to Havana for a short vacation and would be back in a few days.

"Why didn't they say goodbye?" he asked her.

"They didn't want to wake you," she answered.

As the days and weeks passed, he finally said, "I know that they are not coming back. They left Cuba to meet Bertico (my father) and we will never see each other again, right? I will never be able to travel, and by the time *they* are able to come back, I will not be alive."

Having guessed what had happened, my grandmother told him the truth and comforted him as best she could. However, over the next few weeks he became severally depressed. He stopped eating, taking his walks, and eventually stayed in bed almost all day. Not long after, he had a stroke and eventually heart failure ended his life.

My mom never forgave herself for the decision she made. "I know it was my fault," she always said. But my mom had made the right choice, to move forward with both her life and mine. I watched her sacrifice everything. Her inspiration and self-empowerment stirred the same passion in my heart. A passion I would find the strength to use later in my life.

~Imprisonment~

After eleven months, the time had finally come to continue our journey. The arrangements to travel from Cuba to Panama were not legal and neither were the ones to travel to the United States. We had to be very careful, cautious, and smart. We said goodbye to our new found friends in Panama. It had been a bittersweet stay; yet, as we said farewell, the overwhelming feeling of abandonment and loss returned.

We arrived at the airport nervous and apprehensive. Holding hands, we walked towards the gate. Suddenly uniformed Panamanian government officers intercepted us. They pulled us apart and took my mother to a room. "*Mimi!*" I hollered as they took her away. The officer held me tight and I lost sight of her.

I had no idea that my mom had become a prisoner. I just thought that she was being detained for questioning. I was brought back to the house with the little room. When I arrived, I saw the owner of the house and her neighbors waiting. I walked in and asked, "Is Mimi here?"

They all looked at each other as to who should be the one to speak. Finally, the owner of the house said, "There is something we need to tell you about your mom."

I started backing away and screamed as loud as I could. All the emotions that I had pent up since I was 4 years old came out of me. I screamed, I cried, I fought against the kind people who tried to hold me, to console me. I had lost so many people and so much in my life, but this feeling of losing my mom was beyond my comprehension.

"Did she die?!" I kept asking. "*Where is my mom!*" I demanded. "Where is she? I want to see her!" I was hyperventilating and hysterical.

"No, *niña*, your mom is in jail for a few days; she'll be fine," she said.

"But I want to see her! Can you take me?" I begged.

"We can't, Xiomara. They don't allow minors in the facility."

I kept thinking of my mom in a jail cell-images from seeing television shows and reading comic books of what a cell looks like popped into my mind. I had a million questions. Is my mother wearing one of those prisoner uniforms? Is she eating? Is she alone or with others? But no one knew the answers.

I was told that I was now in Panamanian custody and that neither I nor my mother would not be released until my dad sent a relative from Miami to bail us out.

They settled me down and I was fed and put to bed. I had some routine during the day, mostly worrying about my mom and what was going to happened. But the nights were the worst. *"What was going through my mom's mind? How was she feeling?"* And I asked God for strength, wondering, "How much more can she and I take?" But the hardest question I asked was of myself— how was it that I could have been so blind as not to see her deep love and devotion to me? I finally understood why my mother continuously said to me whenever I would take my father's side in Cuba, "Xiomara, you don't know what it is to be a mother; wait and one day you will see."

CHAPTER 5

THE BLACK HOLE

A nother try. This was our second attempt to get to the USA. It is now or never. If we tried and failed, this time my mom will be convicted and jailed in Panama. Our plan was to travel to Mexico and from there cross the border into Texas; into freedom.

We needed to get through the airport screening process once again and the pressure and emotions were even greater this time. An employee at the airport patrol noticed how nervous we looked and was suspicious at first, but after a few tense moments of conversation with my mother, he realized how vulnerable we were and decided to help us pass through without any interrogation. And after about twenty minutes were at the gate; soon on the plane and flying to Mexico City.

I wondered why we were suddenly so lucky. Why did that man help us? Though I'll never know for certain, my belief is that he his soul was touched by an angel. Once again, God was watching over us.

We arrived in Mexico and went directly to a small hotel and paid in advance for the room. We had no idea how long we would be there.

From our window, I saw that there was a beautiful park right in front of the hotel, with dark green grass, a myriad of flowers, and a beautiful fountain. I asked my mother, "Can I look at the fountain? I will be right back and I promise no one will see me!"

She looked at me and gave me a small nod. I ran quickly to and twice around the fountain. I dragged my hand in the pool of water at its base. I walked over and bent down to touch the soft grass. I walked over and stared at the sunlit flowers. God was so generous with me to allow this gift. But, the sun was beginning to set and we knew I had to run back to the hotel. Soon it would be time to move on.

Before we could cross the border, we'd be contacted by the "coyotes," smugglers who specialize in sneaking illegal aliens into the U.S. A few hours later, there was a furious knock on our door, a whispered command to follow the man standing in the hallway, and my mother and I grabbed our small suitcases and walked out of the hotel. We followed him to a few blocks, down an alley and saw several men standing with a group of women, standing by an old Volkswagen van. Coyotes make their money smuggling groups, not individuals, and our group included four other teenage girls, an older woman, and my mother. "Into the van," a surly man ordered, and we all obeyed. I was nervous, but also excited. Soon my mother and I would be at the border.

"When will we get there?" I asked my mother. She shrugged her shoulders and whispered to me to be quiet. Around eleven in the morning, after several hours on the road, we saw a road sign— "Reynosa, 30 km." "Is that were we're going?" I asked. My mother nodded and put her finger to her lips. I smiled at her and became silent. We drove through the streets of the city and into an area of ramshackle houses and the van pulled into a dark garage, lit only by the vans headlamps. The man sitting by the driver hopped out and opened the side panel of the van.

We all stood there in the dark. I held my mother's hand. I could feel her muscles tense. Suddenly a bright light shined in our eyes and we heard the man with the flashlight say, "Double. If you want to continue, you need to pay us double!" The older woman began to protest, but he slapped her in the face and yelled at her to shut up.

"Each of you will be allowed one phone call to get the money," he said. We looked at each other, bewildered and stunned and several people began to cry.

"None of that!" he shouted, and we were herded into small room in the back of the garage. There was one bare bulb hanging from the ceiling, barely lighting the room. One by one, the women and their children were let out to make their phone call. Two of the younger girls came back sobbing. The older woman went out with her daughter and we could hear shouting. My mother pressed her ear to the door to listen.

It seemed that whoever the woman called didn't have the money and one of the coyotes decided how she could pay. My mother listened in shock as the woman screamed while her daughter was dragged away and the men began to laugh.

My mother backed away from the door, hearing approaching sobs, just as the door flung open and the older woman was thrown to the floor. The man looked at us, huddled together and scared beyond words. He just smiled at us and the said, "See? Money or rape, your choice," and slammed the door behind him.

The older woman lay on the dirt floor of our little hell, trembling, sobbing, and yelling unintelligibly as people from our group held her down.

I sometimes still hear the haunting screams of the girl. I shudder to think that that could've been me.

My mother beat on the door and pleaded for mercy from the coyotes.

"Shut up!" a voice hollered. But my mother continued to holler for mercy. Suddenly the door opened and a sneering man pointed a pistol at her, "You, come here!" he said.

I held on to one of her legs and would not let go.

"Xiomara," she pleaded, "don't do this, they will kill us. I will be back." I was more afraid of losing her than anything else. I sobbed uncontrollably, my imagination wild with horrible thoughts. I kept praying to God for her safe return. More than an hour passed when the door opened and my mother was thrown onto the floor.

I ran to her and turned her on her back, hugging her as I did so. "What happened Mimi?" I asked tearfully. "Did they hurt you?"

With a faltering voice, she said, "No *mi Vida*, they just wanted me to call your dad. It took forever for the call to go through."

"Is he coming to get us?" I asked, just as the door was thrown open.

"Everyone shut up!" one of the Coyotes screamed before my mother could answer. "I will kill every one of you if you keep talking! Go to sleep!" He threw in a few thin, tattered blankets and just before he stepped back through the door, the young girl they had raped was dumped back into the room. Her mother ran to her, hugged her, but the girl pushed her away. She crawled to a corner of the room, away from the light, sat there, her arms wrapped around her curled knees and sobbed.

"Mimi?" I began to ask my mother what had happened, but she just shook her head and held me close. As she gently rocked me, I felt a tear fall from her cheek to mine. "Go to sleep, Xiomara" she whispered and we lay close together on the chilly floor.

Within an hour, most people were asleep from sheer emotional exhaustion. I tried to sleep, but couldn't. I was cold; there wasn't enough thin blankets for everyone and I hadn't scrambled fast enough to get one for me and my mother. I laid there asking God to tell me how long this nightmare would last and what would happen to my mother and me?

A few minutes later the door began to open slowly and a young man stepped into the room. He quietly closed the door behind him and turned to us, gently kicking a few people to wake them. He kept his finger to his lips to indicate that we all should be silent. I shook my mother awake and we stared at the young man, wondering what would happen next. Was another of us to be raped? Was he there to shoot one of us?

He removed the finger from his lips and whispered, "I'm going to help you, but you must do as I say."

"I'm going to say this only one time. I've got to get all of you out of here at 3:00 a.m. If anyone makes a sound, we are all going to die. Is that clear? 3:00 a.m.-be ready," the Coyote commanded. The better watches had already been stolen by the coyotes, but one of the ladies had an old Timex. She looked at her watch in the dim light, and whispered back, "We'll be ready!"

Our relatives had been given a midnight deadline to get the money deposited and I guess they had.

At exactly 3:00 a.m., he and his buddy tied down the gate guard and slowly got us out, one by one. We were loaded into the van and driven to the border.

Coyotes only have loyalty to each other, not to the poor souls they smuggle. "A coyote who betrays a coyote, is a dead man!" was their motto. They have left groups stranded in the desert or shot them dead after they had been paid. Money was the sole reason they smuggled.

It was much later that we found out that our coyote and his partner had begun to secretly negotiate with our family members. Money was to be sent into an account where he could monitor the deposits. Money ruled, and if he and his buddy could score and cut out the others, all the better.

But on our way a tire blew. We were ushered out of the van to act as lookouts while the two men changed the tire. The young girl who had been raped now stood silently, staring at the men with hatred, her fists clenched. He mother comforted her as best she could, whispering to her to stay quiet.

Because of the flat, we could not cross the border within the right time frame. So our coyotes herded us into us inside a container they had on site, one so small that it seemed impossible that we would all fit. We squeezed together knowing that if we could not make room enough for everyone, there is no question that the Coyotes would kill any who didn't fit.

We had to press tightly against each other. There was no space to bend our legs and hardly any space to move from side to side. The men left a small part of the door open so we could get some air, but there was still not enough for everyone to breathe comfortably and I often felt that I would pass out. Even in the desert cold of night, crowded as were, it became sweltering. I realized that if I had passed out from either lack of air or the heat, I'd still be standing, as we were so crowded I would have no place to fall.

And worst of all, there wasn't enough water for everyone. The coyote's had only given us two small canteens of water so everyone just took a sip to make the water last; that is to say, those who were lucky enough to be able to move their arms to get one of the canteens.

We were in the container so long that a few of the women urinated or defecated on themselves and the smell became unbearable. And, like the punch line to the joke about "it couldn't be worse," it began to rain. A hard, torrential rain. The sound of the rain hitting the container was both deafening and agonizing as we all wanted to be outside, with space enough to dance amongst the rain, cool off and open our mouths to drink in the precious water.

I closed my eyes tightly and prayed. In my mind I heard, "*I am here. Stay strong Xiomara.*"

After a time—how long it was I never found out, a lifetime, it seemed—the door of the container was opened and, though the light was blinding, I could see another van, side-door open, a few steps away.

One of the men waved his pistol and we were escorted to the awaiting van. The rain felt cold, but refreshing. Before we stepped into the van, the other man let each of us take a long sip from a large water jug he had placed by the door.

Once we were all in the van, we felt a relief and calm that announced God's presence and His angels, protecting each one of us. We drove for about an hour before the van stopped at the foot of a mountain, and we were told to get out to begin a final journey on foot.

The rain was coming down hard, making the surface of the mountain muddy and difficult to walk. My mother and I were about the middle of the group as we headed up what was supposed to be a trail. People took a few steps and then were slipping back down. But everyone soldiered on. All we needed to do was to climb the mountain and touch US territory, we were told. Just follow the trail. I helped my mother along, and then she'd help me. We all stepped up to the task, though at times it seemed an effort in muddy futility. Still, the reward of freedom, the chance to start a new life, made every difficult step worthwhile.

The rain began to slow and the coyote who had been leading us stepped aside and told us to continue, as he had to talk with his partner. We trudged on and as we passed him he waved his gun and urged us "Go on; go on! You're almost there! Just a little further!" After a few minutes, my mother turned and looked at the people behind us. Everyone was there, except the coyotes. They had abandoned us.

My mother looked about, wondering what to do. I watched her raise her face to the sky and I knew that she was asking God for help. She grabbed my hand. All we could do was walk on. I felt the strength of her conviction, knowing that as she led my hand, God was holding hers. I started yelling at everyone to give them strength, too. I was just a 12-year old girl-but something (or someone) within me gave me the power for people to listen. "You are going to die if you don't push yourself up! Everyone go up the mountain! Do it now! We can make it! Think of your family! Let's go!" But, as we trudged on it was becoming more and more difficult for everyone, we were wearing out, especially my mother.

"*Mi Amor no puedo. No puedo.*" she kept saying. It was at this point that I had a true "out of body" experience. In that instant, I floated above and saw myself and my mother on that mountain trail.

A voice other than my own came out when I spoke. I started ordering her, "Give me your right arm!"

I half-pushed, half-carried her to the top of that mountain. Others saw me and took heart. I pushed her from her back, agonizing over each step. I gave her my all until I was too spent and exhausted. But, there was no time to spare. I heard the sound of whistles and knew that the authorities were coming. Perhaps we had been spotted, or the coyotes had betrayed us, since they now had their money. It was enough to get what little strength I had to get up and over the mountain.

I found myself in the unexpected role of protecting my mother. There is only one explanation for the strength I had suddenly found; it was a miracle of Faith and of Hope. From that point on I realized that my life was about being strong and not giving up; becoming a woman and leaving the girl behind. Understanding God's plan and sharing the faith and hope I had found, with others.

We walked down the mountain just before sunset and were met by another group of coyotes. One of them men called out my mothers and another woman's name and we found ourselves being separated from our group. We three began to panic until an elderly woman approached us and asked us to follow her. I asked what was going to happen to us and she explained that while the others would be taken to a quiet spot along the Rio Grande and had to make their way illegally into the United States, our relatives had secured papers for us. She was a member of a group of charity workers who worked reluctantly worked with the coyotes and whose mission it was to welcome *gusanos* like us and help us get into the U.S. They gave us food, water, a shower, and our papers. Whatever else our two coyotes were, they did as they had promised and got us where we needed to go.

CHAPTER 6

A MONSTER
OUT OF THE CAGE

hat does he look like now? Am I going to recognize him? What do we talk about? So many questions ran through my mind as we prepared to cross the Mexican Border into McAllen, Texas. I scanned the crowd at the passport control from a distance. My heart leapt. I saw my *papi* standing and watching us.

The look on the immigration authorities faces, the cold, sterile facilities, and the questions we were asked was like the others we had experienced before. Although we had showered, our clothes were spotted in mud stains. I felt self-conscious and felt a shiver go up my spine. I looked anxiously at my mother. I felt trapped in the room as if we were criminals. I waited, and hoped that this time it might be different. I held my breath until I heard the thud of the custom officers' stamp on the small piece of paper. It was over! We were finally legal entrants to the place I had dreamed about for so long, the United States of America.

The moment the doors opened and we were allowed to pass through my father was standing with his arms opened wide. He stood there, right in front of me, and I had no idea what to say to him. Of course, I loved him, but my feelings and the "good father" image was gone. We had both been through so much, and nothing was the same. Yes, I still loved him…but I didn't *like* him.

He stood there awaiting my response and I did the same. I was more mature now. I was more confident. But when our eyes met, I ran towards him as though I was four-years-old again. I couldn't help it. I was swiftly wrapped in his strong, familiar embrace. I cried and whispered to him, "*Papi,* promised me you will never leave me again."

That first night we stayed with a "good Samaritan" woman in her farm house. I didn't want to fall asleep, afraid that if I woke up it would have all been a dream.

I could barely keep my eyes open, but I stayed next to him to make sure that he would not leave. I was happy but cautious at the same time. I needed to know what would happen next.

I closed my eyes and pretended to sleep so that my parents would begin talking. I wanted to hear the truth of what was going to happen and knew they would not talk in front of me. They did begin to talk, whispering to each other. I couldn't quite hear what they were saying, but I knew that I would be devastated if he would leave us again. I tried to stay awake to hear them, but sleep overcame me. As I drifted away, said a silent prayer and had hope and faith that the next day the sun would rise and a new day, and new beginning, was just ahead for us.

~Living in America~

Life in Cuba was different from life in Panama, and Mexico, and greatly different from life in the United States. In Cuba, we didn't have much food, hardly anything to wear, and obviously, no freedom. So my expectations of American life were very high; and I wasn't disappointed. "The sky is the limit and a dream can become a reality!" I believed. I would say to my mother, "I'm going to eat everything I see!"

"Look what I brought for you," said our "good Samaritan" hostess. She was holding a flimsy, white cardboard box that had a transparent "window" in the middle. I looked in and saw big circular pieces of something.

"What's inside the box?" I asked.

She used her fingernail to cut open the small piece of tape that kept the lid closed, opened the box and said, "These are donuts. You never had them before? Try them. You'll love them!"

"They look tempting," I said in a tiny voice. I was so hungry; my stomach was rumbling. She smiled at my hesitation to take one. I kept looking at the donuts and my mouth watered. I picked one up, took a few small bites and put it down.

"You didn't like them?" She sounded disappointed.

"I really want to eat more, but I can't; I feel so full," I said as my voice started to crack. I was on the verge of crying. I was scared that something had damaged my stomach.

My dad reminded me that we had not eaten for several days during the time we were kidnapped and my mother said, "Xiomara, what's happening to you is normal. Your stomach has shrunk from lack of food.

Don't worry," she said, giving me a reassuring hug, "little, by little, it will get back to normal."

I nodded and thanked our benefactor. She closed the box and said, "They're here when you want some more," as she headed into the kitchen.

I looked around her big country house, so beautiful and peaceful. During the day, the bright sunlight would fill the room from the large windows. Looking through them, I could see that the land on which the house stood was so vast that you could not see any other homes. *"How far away were her neighbors?"* I wondered. After all, I was from a small, cramped village in Cuba and no one—except the government—had such a large piece of land just for a house! A white wooden fence surrounded the house proper and beyond that, the cows and other farm animals were free to roam. As was I, with a freedom I had never known.

It wasn't until many years later that I truly appreciated how blessed we were to have this lady, the owner of the farm, in our lives. She was another angel sent by God, and she made our first experience in the U.S. a little slice of heaven. After all that we had been through, for us there was no place closer.

* * * * *

I had a definite image of how the United States would look. A big city with many lights, tall buildings, lots of stores, things to do and outdoor activities, and close to the beach—a postcard-perfect setting.

"Mimi, I am confused. Are we really in the United States?" I asked my mother. "'cause this isn't what I thought it would be like."

"Yes," she replied, "we are in the United States, but this is a rural area outside the city. You will get to see the city soon."

Indeed, in a week we were heading to our new home in Miami. I was no longer afraid of an airplane anymore and enjoyed watching the land from the window. Flying over Florida, all I saw was bright sunshine and puffy clouds. I was sitting next to my dad and I couldn't stop smiling! It felt like a big, magical world, a magical city, and a magical moment— perfect.

~Papi's Real Life~

Like many immigrants, before we could afford a place of our own, we lived at a relative's house. Here in Miami it was my cousin's house, a person that we barely knew, and once again, we all had to share another small room.

{The claustrophobic issues I experienced in Panama returned. Additionally, we had no idea who was the homeowner.}

The first night in our small room was a nightmare. Thinking I was asleep, my mom and dad began to argue about where we were going to stay after this. "You have been here for several years, Bertico," my mother said. "You have to have a home!" My father didn't answer.

He was telling her that there was no other place to stay for the time being. She wondered why he hadn't made other arrangements. I pretended to awaken and they stopped arguing.

My father looked at me. "Xiomara and you will be staying here until I get a place for all of us to move into…together. I'll be back tomorrow."

I looked at him, my eyes beginning to tear, "What do you mean *Papi*?" I asked. He was going to walk out again? This can't be happening! "Where are you going? Momma and I don't know these people we're staying with. Please, *Papi*, don't go!" He didn't say anything, and turned around to go. I had to say something to get him to stay, and so I said the words that devastated me, "I thought you loved me more than anything!"

Slowly he turned towards me and said, "I promised you that we will be together, and here we are. I will be back tomorrow and show you both what my life is like here, my job, and where I stay."

I cried as he walked out of the room, and more so when I heard the front door close behind him.

I eagerly waited for him to arrive the next day. I watched out the window for hours until I saw a van pull into the driveway. I wondered who it was, until I saw the driver's side door open and my father step out.

As promised, he picked my mother and me up and took us to see where he worked. As we drove, he told me that the company sign he had painted on the van was his own design. I was so proud of him, seeing that he was the same creative and talented father I had in Cuba, that I began to forget the worst part about him.

When we arrived at his small studio, my mother and I walked around and looked at his paintings. It was so interesting to see them here in Miami. I remembered the small table in our house in Cuba, where he had created his beautiful artwork and had become so famous. I was happy that he still had his talent and that a new audience could see his work. Still, I was curious about other things.

"*Papi*, can we go now, so you can show me the city, and your house?" I asked. "Where do you live? Can you take us to see it?" He turned his head toward my mother. He couldn't look me in the eyes.

I grabbed a paintbrush and started playing with a big canvas, pretending that the dry brush had paint on it. He came close to me and pulled up a small bench. He watched me for a few moments and then gently grabbed my hand and took the brush. He looked blankly at me.

"This...," he said, glancing at my mother and then looking at me, "this is all I have Xiomara. I have no home. I live here."

I looked from him to my mother, but neither of us spoke. My mother shook her head in bewilderment and disappointment, and walked to a chair and sat down. She began to sob quietly.

"But *Papi*," I asked with a young girls lack of understanding, more curious about the small studio, "where do you shower? And there's no kitchen here-where do you eat?

I saw that his face was turning red with embarrassment but he answered, "I take a shower with a hose," he said, "and here..." He got up and showed me a thin mattress hiding behind a wall in the office, "This is where I sleep. My kitchen? Sometimes I eat food out of a can."

"This is why I took us to your cousin's house," he said sadly. "I don't have a home because I have no money left."

My mother looked up at him with a scowl.

"I saved the money to bring you here, as I promised," he said, "and sent you everything you needed in Cuba. But just when I had saved enough money to get you a place to stay, I had to pay the ransom money to the damned Mexican Coyotes. I had the first payment the Coyotes demanded, but for the second one I had to borrow the money."

My mother continued to stare at him. He looked at her and said, "I need some time to make things right." I looked at my mother and I knew that she didn't believe him.

I touched his shoulder and he turned toward me. "No *Papi*," I said, "I'm not leaving you here alone. I'll stay here. We had less than this in Cuba; and I don't mind taking a shower with a hose!"

Even before I heard my mother say, "No you won't!" I knew that it was impossible. I knew that everything he had sacrificed so much to bring us here and I was so confused. It was as though I was a younger child again: he was still my hero and anything he said I believed and agreed with. Yet, in my heart I knew that now we'd begin a different relationship and we'd bond in a different way.

~A different world~

I celebrated my thirteenth birthday in Miami. I was mature enough to realize that though my Dad had no money, we never seemed to lack for anything. I wasn't certain how this happened, just that it did. I found out later that he managed to do it by saving money from his few paying jobs or by bartering his artistic talents for food, clothing, furniture, and whatever we needed at the time.

My mother had a difficult time with the circumstances of our life here and I knew her anger and disappointment was caused by my father. I often heard them quietly arguing, or step outside to argue more loudly. Yet, one thing I remember about this time…

I had two pairs of shoes and the bottom of one pair was coming apart. I would drag my leg slowly so that my *papi* would not see it because I knew that if he did, he'd want to buy me a new pair and I didn't want him to spend any money. But one day, I was walking and he noticed my weird walk and asked me directly why I walked that way. I had to show him my shoe.

"You are my little girl," he said, "and I don't want to see you again like that." He drove me to a shoe store where he was painting a mural. He asked me to wait by the counter and he spoke to the owner.

A moment later he came over to me and said, "Pick anything you want, Xiomara. Whatever you want."

I looked around quickly, picked only one pair and placed them on the counter. "*Papi*, this one is good," I said. He looked at me and called me outside. I thought I had done something wrong.

"When I told you to pick whatever you wanted, I meant as many shoes as you like. You only picked one pair of shoes." I looked at him but said nothing.

"I love you, and I realize all the bad times I made you go through when you were a little girl, but you just taught me a lesson and I am grateful for that." I didn't know what he meant. Seeing the look in my eyes, he explained.

"You were so thoughtful, so very humble, choosing one cheap pair of shoes to save me money. You didn't think I knew what you were doing, but I did. Despite everything, you still love your *papi*. But it's okay. I spoke with the owner and he'll give me a break on the price and simply take it out of my commission. Now, let's go inside and get you some decent *zapatos*!"

I was so very happy at how he had seemed to be a changed man. More caring and responsible. But I soon found that I was mistaken.

For from that time forward, whenever there was an argument between him and my mother, he would say, "Xiomara is the only one of you who loves me-the only one that is with me!" He was using what we had shared as a tool, a weapon against my mother whenever they argued.

It made me feel very guilty, but I also realized that I could use this to my advantage.

~The Bewitching Hour~

I was placed in middle school, but my English was very poor, and I tried to learn as best I could. It didn't help that I sometimes fell asleep during class. Those Cubans who had arrived long before me, now made fun of their "poor, dumb" immigrant girl.

They didn't understand that I couldn't sleep at home. Things had gone from bad to worse and I stayed awake to protect my mother; I had to keep my father from hitting her.

I remember we had a large white clock on the wall, near the front door. My mother and I would watch it every afternoon, just waiting for the time that he would come home. From five to seven at night he would be drinking and I would hold my breath waiting for him, and hearing him walk up to the door, we'd run to our rooms.

Sometimes he'd fumble with the key for so long, that he'd simply sit by the front door and fall asleep without ever entering. It was safe then to get him and put him to bed. Sometimes he managed to make it into the house and collapse on the sofa. But other times it was a demon who walked through the front door.

"Donde esta mi perra?" ("Where is my bitch!") "Come out of the room you coward!" he would demand. His words slammed my mother harder than his fists ever could. If my mother didn't answer him, he would pound on the door and threaten to break it down and drag her out.

"*Papi*, leave her alone-come with me," I would say, gabbing his arm and steering him away.

"Get me something to eat, *mi vida*, and my rum" he would say. Rice, beans, and rum where his preferred dinner. He'd then usually watch television for a few minutes before falling into a drunken sleep. I'd watch him just lying there, never sure if he would go my mother again that night. I'd sit up until one or two in the morning, to afraid to even go to the bathroom and leave him alone.

* * * * *

My father was a man of contrasts. A demon when drunk, but possessed of wonderful talents when sober. Besides being a gifted artist, he had a very nice singing voice and played several musical instruments. He even recorded an album that occasionally played on local radio. So on those nights when he was only half-drunk but ready to fight, I would distract him by asking him to play the guitar while I sang. This would go on until after midnight. He never cared that I was just a young teenager who needed to wake up early in the morning for school. It never even crossed his mind. It was just that I was there with him, and that was all he cared about.

It continued to spiral. Saturdays were the worst because he only worked a half day, so was able to spend more time with drinking with his buddies. It also meant that we were never certain just when he'd come home. The fear and anxiety of the unexpected started getting worse for us when he would not pay the electric bills and the electricity was routinely disconnected. Same with the water.

He always blamed my mother. "You are nothing! You are a *BITCH*!" He'd scream as he drunkenly swung his fist at my mother.

"*Hay, Hay, Hay, Xiomara! Corre, corre, me quiere matar!*" (Hurry, Hurry, Hurry, Xiomara! He is going to kill me!) She would desperately shriek as she ran through the house with him lumbering after her. I was the twelve-year-old peacemaker that had to keep things reasonably quiet. And worse, he often had me accompany him to the bars, to hang out with him and his friends, just as I had done when he had had his friends visit us when I was a small girl in Cuba. But now, my job really wasn't to be the cute daughter he was proud of, it was to be sure he got home when he was way too drunk. It was no life for either myself or my mother.

"Why me, Mimi?" I'd ask my mother. "Why can't I be just like my friends? Have a normal life?"

"Because your father only listens to you, Xiomara," she'd respond sadly. You have to be twelve going on forty." She paused and added, "You have no idea how often I wish we could go back to Cuba. I should have listened to your *Abuelo's* advice to not follow your dad."

She looked blankly at the wall, recalling his words. "Barbara, please don't go to meet Bertico, he will destroy your life and you will have no one to help you," she said and added, "I should have listened. This really isn't the kind of life I thought it would be." She curled her lips in a half-smile and took my hand in hers, "For either of us."

We endured as best we could, but as months passed by, our financial situation became worse. My father felt the pressure of having to provide for us and that made him drink even more. The angrier he got with himself, and his life in general, the worse the fighting became. Words and threats, the verbal abuse was bad enough, but, though my mother tried to cover it up, the occasional physical abuse became something to deal with. He'd always apologize when he was sober, it would never happen again, he just couldn't understand why he acted this way, just a while longer, he was changing! But it was obvious that we were a bother in his life. Whatever he thought our being together would be like was not what it actually was. He had managed to live as he wanted before we came. Now he couldn't. And he felt that he only had himself to blame, since he was the one who brought us here. Before then, the demon had been held in check. He had kept it locked up. But now, the monster had been released from its cage.

* * * * *

~ THE STORM ~

If he hadn't gone out with a friend, I sometimes had to go with him. So, this was my life as a young teen, out on the town-not for myself or with my friends, but with my father at one of his clubs.

"Look, this is my daughter!" he would exclaim, put his arm around me into a side hug. And then he'd ruin the moment by saying something like, "Look how fast she can drink this beer! She is just like me!" His friends would just laugh. I was not only his entertainment but his friends also. Yes, indeed, he was very proud of me. It was embarrassing, but expected of me. I was his caretaker; his minder. And the hardest part was getting him to leave, getting him home, and getting him to sleep. Sometimes he insisted on driving home, which scared me witless, but usually I was able to convince him to let me drive— underage and unlicensed. I know that God guided me home every time I drove. And I always said a prayer of thanks for mi abuelo for letting me sit on his lap and "learn" how to drive when I was a small child in Cuba. Brake, gas, drive, reverse and park, turn the wheel gently, drive the car-don't let it drive you! Sometimes living in a rural area trumps the big city!

* * * * *

"Mimi, Papi has not come home yet and it is already 11:00 p.m., do you think something has happened to him?"

"No Xiomara-go to sleep. He probably being dropped off or stayed with a friend. He might have fallen asleep in the workshop. You go to sleep."

But, that was impossible. At 4:00 a.m., I said to her, "Mimi, don't you think we should go to sleep? He is taking longer and I need to get up for school in three hours." I went to my room and crawled into bed, but my inner voice told me not to fall asleep.

About twenty minutes later, I heard my father come into the house. He wasn't yelling or making noise, he walked to the bedroom door, jimmied the lock, quietly walked to my mother's side of the bed and grabbed her by her hair and dragged he into the living room! She awoke with a fright and screamed, *"Hay Bertico, Hay Bertico, dejame, no me hagas eso!"* (Bertico, Bertico, let me go, don't do this to me.)

I scrambled out of bed and ran into the living room. The front door was open and I stepped outside. I felt like everything was moving in slow motion. I looked around and couldn't see anyone at first, but then I saw my father standing by the pool. I began to run to him and as I got closer, I saw my mother floating in the pool. She had never learned to swim!

"Mimi! Mimi!" I hollered and jumped into the pool to rescue her. She was already slowly sinking. I tried my best to pull her up, but she was heavy for me and as much as I was trying to save her, she was pulling me down with her. I prayed for strength and my prayer was answered. With a few strong strokes and a mighty heave, I was able to bring her to the surface, and lift her out of the water. I looked for my father, thinking he would be there to help, but he was gone. I rolled her on her side, and she began to cough out some water. She then managed to speak through her tears, "I told you, Xiomara, I told you! He wants to kill me...and I know he will!" She coughed up the last of the water, and felt strong enough to sit up.

"No Mimi," I said, "he's not going to kill you. Do you hear me! We are going to leave this house and we are going to be safe." She nodded and began to stand up.

My mother held on to me as we went into the house, not just because she was still a little unsteady, but for support if my father came at her again. But the man just sat on the sofa, glaring at us as we walked in. He said nothing, and didn't move.

Our neighbors heard the commotion and called the police. As soon as he heard a car pull up and saw the police lights, my father sprang from the sofa and stood in the corner behind the door.

"Don't you dare say one word of what happened here," he threatened. There was a knocking on the door and as I opened it, I felt his eyes burning into me.

"Who is it I asked?"

"Police, ma'am. We got a call about someone screaming," the officer said.

I thought quickly as I opened the door. "Oh, yes, officer," I said. "My dog fell into the pool and I was screaming to save him."

"Are you sure?" the officer kept asking me, "and what were you doing awake at this hour?"

"I was sleeping, but I heard my dog barking so I got up to see why he was barking."

The two officers looked at each other. "Is he alright, now?" the other officer asked.

"All dried off and happy. It's a good thing I can swim!" I said, once again acting as a frightened little girl.

Again, the two police officers looked at each other.

"Could we talk with your parents?" one asked. I froze for a minute, but then my mother put her hand on my shoulder.

"Sorry to have bothered you, officers," she said. "But that damned dog is a nuisance! She leaned over my shoulder and said, "Next time, just let him drown!"

"For heaven's sake, don't do that!" he said smiling. "We'll let your neighbor know everything is okay."

"If you need anything, anything at all, we will be around in the neighborhood. You can call us anytime," the other officer said.

"Thank you," mother said, "Good night!"

They seemed to sense that something else had happened, but since we denied it, they just let us know they'd be watching.

My father was ashen and shaking and didn't move from the corner for a few minutes, until he heard the police car drive off.

My dad was petrified of the police in general, and more so now. My mother and I went back to our rooms and locked the door. My father stayed in the living room, to make a quick exit if he had to.

Unfortunately, this would not be the last time the neighbors would call the police to come to our house.

CHAPTER 7

THE "BROKEN" HEART

The body can just take so much when it is under stress. I was fifteen years old and taking a shower when, suddenly, I found myself on the floor of the shower stall, my hand clutching a piece of the ripped shower curtain. The warm water was still spraying on my shaking body. What had happened to me? I didn't remember falling or sliding on a piece of soap. I called out to my mother, "Mimi, I...I fainted in the bathroom--I'm shaking and scared!"

My mother screamed when she saw me, worried that I had hit my head. "I'm okay...I think," I said half-heartedly. "Help me up."

"What happened, Xiomara? Did you slip?" she asked as she helped me towel off.

"I'm not sure," I said. "Sometime I have these strange episodes. Once in a while when I stand up, I get dizzy. Maybe that's it." I looked at myself in the mirror. The impact was so hard, that bruises started to appear. The same reddish-purple splotches I had often seen on her.

"Can you get dressed by yourself?" she asked me. But before I could answer she had left the bathroom to grab her purse to take me to the hospital.

After over an hour of filling out forms and waiting, a doctor finally saw us. I explained what happened and he said he'd like someone else to see me. Half an hour later another doctor examined me. "Just avoid taking hot showers and drink lots of liquids until we figure out what caused the incident," advised the neurologist. "But what happened to me?" I asked. "Are you sure that I don't have something going on in my brain that you are not telling me?"

The doctor's advice was to stand up slowly getting out of bed, a chair, the car—anytime I was sitting or lying down. No medicines, just caution—but if it kept happening, come back immediately.

I did as told, making dramatic slow and stately exits from seats at movie theaters, concert halls, and restaurants. I might have appeared a prima donna, but I took care of myself and it became second nature to rise slowly. Years passed without an episode. Then when I was thirty-two years old, despite my caution, it happened again.

This time I was extensively examined and diagnosed with three types of arrhythmia. In those short periods of time when the episodes occurred, oxygen wouldn't reach my brain. They kept asking me questions about my past. Had I had any medical emergencies as a child? Had I ever fallen and hit my head? Had I ever suffered chest pains? What was my childhood home life like?

I told them everything—the verbal and physical abuse I had witnessed at home, my anxious escape from Cuba and my experience kidnapped by the coyotes, the attempted murder of my mother: everything. It was a relief to have had a reason to say it all out loud.

After a few minutes discussion, the doctors believed that it was most likely caused because of the stress I experienced to as a child.Throughout the years, I must have begun showing abnormal symptoms and episodes of fatigue, both of which I had dismissed as nothing important, until it culminated in occasional fainting spells. The original diagnosis of heart arrhythmia was correct and I remain under treatment for it to this day.

As I started researching and discussing my condition with doctors, I learned that people who experienced stressful childhoods might develop diseases related to stress and these constant stressful situations increase the chances of severe illnesses for the rest of their lives. Domestic abuse then can be likened to second-hand smoke in that a child exposed to it suffers as much as the participants.

CHAPTER 8

THE ACCIDENT THAT CHANGED MY LIFE

We always lived in a rental property as we were constantly moving from place to place. This was not because we wanted to but because landlords were tired of hearing complaints from the neighbors about the tumult and noise created by my father's domestic abuse.

In the ninth grade, during the middle of the school year, we had to move out to yet another house. It was a new route for the driver meaning that either she miscalculated the distance between pickups and drop-offs or was simply running late. I was riding with her in the moving vans cab. She came to a busy intersection-the light turned from yellow to red quickly, but she ran it anyway. Too late, she was t-boned by an oncoming car. On impact, my body flew towards the engine, dashboard, and windshield.

I blacked out and slowly came to and heard sirens. The police arrived with an ambulance, and I remember people crowding around me, talking to each other, and gently lifting me onto a stretcher to transport me to the hospital. My mouth was full of liquid. I spit it out, but it filled quickly. All I could taste was blood.

After a ride through traffic, siren screaming, the ambulance arrived at the hospital. They rushed me to the emergency room.

I heard one of the EMT (Emergency Medical Technicians) tell the doctor that my two front teeth had crushed into my palate. One tooth had cracked in half. (Miraculously, a police officer found the other half at the scene and delivered it to the hospital).

And being in "survivor mode," I hadn't even thought about my parents. Were they okay? Where were they?

"We need to operate on her immediately, but we can't use full anesthesia," I heard the surgeon tell my mom. They needed to move quickly-I could barely breathe through my nose and mouth, as the swelling encompassed the entire area and respiratory equipment needed to be used. The doctor stepped aside and my mother gently kissed my forehead. I could feel her warm tears on my skin. A nurse grabbed her elbow and my mother quickly turned and was lead out of the room.

They tied my hands and legs to the chair. I moved and made as many noises as possible to get her to return. *"Mimi, don't leave me! I can't breathe! Why are you walking away?"* But I was only thinking these thoughts. I couldn't speak with the respirator on my face. I prayed as I had never prayed before. I hoped that God would hear me, as He had before.

I watched the doctors gathering all the tools and setting up for the operation. The local anesthesia was not working effectively enough and I could feel what was happening.

Both teeth had to be pulled back into the correct position carefully, so they did not completely break. Once they were aligned, the only way to keep them in position was to use iron stitches. Imagine sewing a piece of clothing, and then inserting the needle from front to back to hold the fabric-this is how they used the iron stitches-from front to back repeatedly, through my upper gum.

Although the pain seemed tolerable during the surgery, and despite the medications I was prescribed afterwards, the pain would later be unbearable.

However, even more unbearable was listening to my dad arguing with my mother on the ride from the hospital a few hours later. From what I could hear, the argument was over some trivial matter and had nothing to do with the accident or me. He argued continuously, mindful of nothing but himself. Finally, my mother screamed at him, "Stop! I have had it! Do you see your daughter! Look at her! She doesn't need this! She can't even cry because any type of movement will make her bleed more and she can hardly breathe as it is!"

He looked in the rearview mirror at me in the back seat. All I could do was plead with my eyes for him to stop. Tears welled up in my eyes. My mouth started hurting. I reached forward and he lifted his right arm, palm up, over the seatback. I held it as tight as I could. I needed him to be the kind, loving man I still had memories of. I was in pain and needed *mi Papi* as much as I once did back in Cuba when I was a little girl.

He finally realized what he was doing. He slid his arm back and I settled into the backseat. He looked in the rearview mirror and smiled at me. He was quiet the rest of the way home. He never apologized, but his silence was an apology of sorts.

It was tough enough getting used to a new place to live let alone only "eating" through a straw for the next three months, and missing school. (Although the last one wasn't all that bad for a kid!)

~Return of the leopard~

Unfortunately, as I half expected but hoped it wouldn't happen, it was impossible for my father to keep that good and loving behavior for long. The abuse continued, but I remained silent—literally unable to say a word. The kitty-cat that had brought me home from the hospital had quickly turned back into a leopard. I could only witness him coming in drunk most nights, argue with my mother, watch his temper explode as he threw dishes and vases. My mind echoed with silent screams.

* * * * *

When it was time to remove the stitches and check if the teeth were in place, I was anxious. It was a panicky mood I hadn't experienced since my kidnapping. The surgery to put the iron pins in place had been painful enough, but over the three months a part of the memory of the pain had faded. Now that the pins were being removed, the memory flooded back.

During the procedure, as the pins were being removed, pieces of skin were pulled off still attached to the metal stitches. I cried, screamed, and struggled, but the pain continued as the surgeon removed the stitches. I thought that I had known pain, that I understood agony. I know realized that when I had comforted others in their pain and agony, I really had no point of reference—until now. I prayed to God to comfort me, to make the pain go away. Of course it didn't. Had God failed me?

As a young girl I might have thought so, but as an adult I realize that the surgeons skill, the nurses compassion, and the pharmacists knowledge of medications were all gifts from God.

I have relied on God and his blessings all of my life and would ask for them again concerning this, because three years later, a cyst began to appear at the injury site. I needed oral surgery again. In fact, to date, I have had seven surgeries to my mouth from this accident.

* * * * *

~Bone to bone~

When I was forty, and one day before my daughter's birthday party, one of my front teeth fell out. I staunched the bleeding, wrapped the tooth in cotton, and drove to the dentist. He discovered that I had I needed to have bone implants immediately or every single tooth in that area would begin to fall out. I was traumatized.

Not only would I need to go through bone implant surgery, but cosmetic surgery as well for symmetry, he explained.

I put off the surgery as long as possible—I certainly wasn't going to let it interfere with my daughter's birthday party! However, I had to get it done.

Two months later, when they performed the surgery they found small pieces of cement from the last procedure inside one tooth, a cyst had developed, and my bone mass was weak or nonexistent. All I could do was put my trust in God's hands and the surgeons' skills. "I'm scared and weak. I am really trying to be positive but I don't know if I can go through it again," I thought. "Let's just get it done." Faith and God were my only salvation, truly a salve, a healing balm on my troubling wounds.

It was a prolonged procedure that took several months and many visits to complete. My mother was my strength through all of this. She traveled all the way from Miami, on the East Coast of Florida, to Marco Island, on the West Coast, where I lived, and took care of my daughter and me through my lengthy recovery.

To this day, I'm still unable to eat using my front teeth. I eat and drink using the sides of my mouth and everything needs to be cut into small pieces for me to chew. And no matter how strong I pretend to be, thinking about the procedure still makes me cry. However, I had the comfort of an angel, my mother, and the optimism that God would see me through. I continue to walk with God leading my way and follow His path. He's holding me in his arms, every minute of my life.

CHAPTER 9

THE SMALL WHITE CHURCH

1 Corinthians 2:9 KJV, "But as it is written, Eye hath not seen, nor ear heard, neither have entered into the heart of man, things which God hath prepared for them that love Him."

I have always liked to speak to others about God, one way or another. I see miracles around me every day and I like to point them out when I can. I believe that God has something in store for me. And that He is going to do great things through me. As a teenager, I kept wondering what it was.

I had just turned sixteen, driving alone in my old car when I stopped at a stop sign in a middle of a residential area. There were the usual smattering of houses and to the left of the stop sign, there was a small white church. It was nothing special arcitechturally speaking. Nothing to mark it out of the ordinary, but something about it drew may attention.

I made the left turn and pulled into the church parking lot. It seemed odd to me that I felt a compulsión to be there. I stayed in the car and wondered what would happen if I entered the church. After a few minutes, my curiosity got the better of me and I prayed that it was God guiding me as I got out of the car and walked to the entrance.

The doors were open and I stepped from the bright day into the dark church. After my eyes adjusted, I looked around. The church was empty.

I walked in and sat on the back pew, near the door. It felt comfortable to sit on the smooth wood bench. I looked at the cross in the middle of the rather plain altar. I noted the scent of beeswax candles that hung in the air from years of church services.

From the doorway I heard a soft voice, "Whatever brings you here, 'Welcome to the house of God'," a man's voice said.

I looked toward him and suddenly burst into tears.

"God has sent me and I don't know why," I said. I don't know why I confessed that to a stranger.

He sat next to me and reached for my hand to comfort me. He was dressed casually, but introduced himself as the church pastor. Church denomination did not concern me. This was a spiritual moment.

I explained that I was uncertain of the path God had chosen for me and we talked for about an hour. He made me feel comfortable and didn't discuss doctrine or belief, only that God has a plan for each of us and coming to realice that and seek to understand that was a wonderful thing. I felt relieved and strentghened. I thanked him and left, he said I would always be welcome there.

I would indeed visit, and every time, we would talk on the same bench. Over time I felt comfortable enough to share both my story and my thoughts. He'd give me Bible messages to guide me through and then I would leave.

Things were no better at home and one day, when recalling how my father almost drowned my mother, I felt overwhelmed and rushed to the church. It was a Wednesday, around five thirty in the evening and I walked right up to the altar, and stood staring at the cross. I felt tears trickle and then flow down my cheeks.

It was too much. I couldn't carry any more of pain I lived with for so many years.

I stood there wondering what might have happened if my father had indeed killed my mother. He'd be in jail, I'd be alone. Where was God in all of that? Oh, God, forgive me! Was I losing my faith?

I was lost in desperate thought when I felt a hand touching my right shoulder. I stood frozen. I felt someone step around me.

Standing in front of me was a blonde haired, green-eyed lady, with a soft and lovely smile. She said nothing, just wrapped her arms gently around me and held me.

I placed my head on her shoulder and whispered, "I'm giving up. My soul is in pain. I'm in a dark hole and I can't seem to get out," I told her without even knowing who she was.

She held me tighter and told me that everything would be all right. She released her hug and walked me to the front pew. She said she was the Pastor's wife and had seen me a few times talking to her husband. She was getting the church ready for the six p.m. choir practice, but we had time to talk. I was relieved to do so.

God did indeed have a plan for me. He had led me to this specific church, at the time I needed it most and had filled it with the right people, to help me begin the process of a new chapter in my life. From that time on, I visited that church every Sunday and would sit in the comfortable pew in the back.

After a few weeks, the pastor asked me if I wanted to attend Bible study and I eagerly accepted. I wanted to join the youth group and participate and learn more about God's word. However, several months later, I realized that the members of the youth group seemed to lose interest and many stopped attending.

I felt—no…I *knew*— that the group could come alive again, and even grow. I thought of the many teenagers I knew, who, like myself, were in need of guidance and would benefit from being part of the group.

Though I had never read the Bible before and was uncertain how to interpret it, I began to see that there were beautiful messages within it that were healing my pain, and could do so for others. I was bold enough to give advice to the Pastor on incorporating activities for the youth besides simply the Bible study. Mixed basketball teams, "horse," game night, even homework help. Over time, the group membership began to increase.

I did not know what a "calling from God" was. And yet, without knowing it, I was feeling God becoming closer and I learned that God was working through me to make a difference in the church. The more I attended the church, the more often I recognizedI glimpses of light within the darkest moments I was living through. This wonderful feeling brought me so much peace and joy, that I could better bear my burdens and look forward to the next day.

It was like sunshine inside my body. It was warm, it was radiant, it made me see beyond myself and my circumstances. It was within me, yet a light above and beyond the sun. Simple things like looking at flowers, feeling the warm air of a summer breeze hitting my face, or watching the clouds slowly move and change shape in the blue sky of autumn seemed new to me again.

It was so powerful, so overwheming, that one day, my legs buckled in the middle of a Sunday service and I knelt and began to weep uncontrollably. "Are you alright?" my startled pew-mate asked.

I looked up at her and said, "I'm not crying out of pain, but out of joy!" I had the sudden realization that, although I had prayed all of my life, and believe that I had heard God speak to me in the quiet of my mind, this was the first time I had felt the spirit of God inside me.

I rose to my feet and after the service was over, I told the pastor what had happened and I asked to be baptized, to make the commitment—as an adult—to receive Jesus as my Savior.

* * * * *

"You're a missionary! You have the gift," the group leader told me. "People trust you and they see you as a leader. Xiomara, go through life thinking this way because He has a job for you to finish."

I knew I had a purpose in life, but as a missionary?

"God knows how to select His children based on their abilities. He knows yours and He will let you know when you are ready to use them," he concluded.

I eventually moved away and left that particular church. But I never forgot what I had found there or the words of the group leader.

~A Revelation~

Soon after I experienced the true love of God, and shared that experience with my mother, she too began to find her strength of belief increase and found the courage to finally move out of the house and away from my father. We rented a small apartment but it was a paradise to be away from the almost nightly torments we had suffered. But, it did not take long for my father to find us and to begin to try and persuade my mother to take him back.

"Lo *siento* (I'm sorry)" he would plead, crocodile tears in his eyes. Though perhaps he really meant it this time—perhaps not. He would change. See?—and he'd brandish a bottle of rum and empty the few sips remaining on the sidewalk, then throw the bottle into the bushes. My father was an artist and gave dramatic flair to everything he did. "You need me, *mi vida*," he'd say. "You know that you can't make it without me. I saved every penny to bring you and Xiomara here. I've been bad, I know it—but I need you…and you need me!"

I watched my mother start to waiver. She wasn't falling for it, was she?

"Mimi, if you found the strength and we are finally free from harm, why would you take him back? We have jobs and we can take care of ourselves," I reminded her.

"It's not that simple, Xiomara. I'm afraid of being alone, raising a teenage daughter, and every time he comes around he makes me feel that I'm worthless without him. I'm scared," she replied.

I tried to reassure her as best I could.

"It's going to take only one more fight, Mimi, one more bruise, for you to make your decision," I said. "I know that you will find the courage to walk away. I just hope it won't be too late."

My *abuela* had arrived on a temporary visa to visit us and I was driving to the bakery to get *pastelitios*. I had been in the car just a few minutes, maybe two blocks away, when I felt uneasy. A voice echoed in my head: *"turn back, and do it NOW!"* It was as though I was having a revelation. This had happened so often before and I knew it best to listen.

When I pulled in to the parking space, I saw that a small family group had gathered in front of our apartment door. Maybe they were there to see my grandfather, I thought at first but I sensed that it was for something else.

As I walked closer to them, I heard one of them shout my father's name. The leopard walked amongst us.

Once again my father tried show himself as the king of the house, showing up unexpectedly and uninvited. Ignoring family pleas to just leave.

Everything turned black and my ears buzzed with a high-pitched tone; I felt faint. I was reliving the feelings I had felt before; the awful memory of being on the Mexican border and trying to escape. In a second, as the feeling faded and my eyes adjusted to the scene, I saw my mom struggling to pull away from him. My father held her arm tightly and was reaching to grab her other arm.

"Stop it!" I yelled in a voice deep, guttural and not my own. I had always tried to find the light in the darkness, but now I was filled with a righteous anger. *"No more, Papi! Never again!"*

I faced him for the first time and he released my mother's arm and stood staring at me. He was not expecting me to react as I had. My mother ran to the door and into the crowd.

"I'm calling the police," I said calmly and backed through the door, shutting it behind me.

As I did, I glimpsed him making a dash for the door. But, this time he was not going to get away from justice. For hurricane protection, the doors in southern Florida open out and so I asked my uncles and cousins to hold the door so that my father couldn't push it open.

"This time you are going to prison, *Papi*," I said to myself as I dialed 911.

But the alcohol and adrenalin in his body mixed with his anger and desperation to give him extraordinary strength and he managed to push the door open and run through the stunned crowd.

He cursed everyone as he ran past, glaring a hateful eye at my mother and me. I could barely hear the woman on the phone ask, "What's your emergency?" for his screaming. He ran down the sidewalk like a lunatic, flailing his arms and yelling curses.

"What's your…" I finally heard and interrupted her. "Nothing. Were okay now," I said and ended the call. He had escaped from the police, but more importantly, we escaped from him, forever. We never did see my father again.

* * * * *

From that point on mine and my mother's lives were "normal." Well, as normal as they could be.

Once you have so many emotional scars, it's impossible for them all to disappear. And while there is some truth to the axiom that "Time heals all wounds," unless you allow the divine in you to make you complete you still grapple with the demons of memory that sometimes creep into your thoughts.

For myself, I managed to find work in retail, with the JCPenney department store, part-time at first and then full-time. My mother too found a part-time job and together we tried to heal and rebuild our lives.

My experiences at JCPenney helped me grow personally and professionally. I couldn't quite forget my past, but the memories seemed to become more distant. After I finished high school—something I had always dreamed of doing—I felt emotionally empowered to go to college. My new home life, work experience, and new friends gave me a renewed sense of optimism. But it truly was my belief in God and my three old friends that had helped me along the way: faith, hope, and love.

CHAPTER 10

FAILURE
OR LEARNING
EXPERIENCE?

I went into a transformation when I married for the first time. It was a totally different experience, to be with a man with whom I believed I would spend the rest of my life.

I was just eighteen, staring college, and he was twenty when we first begin our relationship. I was nervous at first, not about him but rather how my mother might react to my having a serious relationship. Luckily, I didn't have to worry. She was happy that I had found my "someone special" and knew that I would never go through what she had. Our families became one.

My boyfriend and I were young and inexperienced, but shared the same characteristics: we loved challenges, taking risks, and were both extremely business oriented. We had it all planned out. In our minds, it was all about studying, graduating college, and starting a business, so we could provide our future children a good life— then retire early to enjoy life ourselves!

We both attended Florida International University. He attended full-time and graduated before we got married. I was a part-time student and graduated a few years after we were married.

He was supportive of both my ambitions and education and covered my school expenses. My mother eventually moved in with us to assist with the house expenses.

It was truly a team effort between myself, my husband, and my mother that made us flourish. At first. Unfortunately, as time went on I began to see cracks appear in our perfect little world.

Between working, studying, and opening and growing our small business, there was no time left for my husbands and my relationship to grow. On the contrary, after a few years what once was our passion, developing our business, became what destroyed our marriage.

I did many things right in our marriage. So did he. I did many things wrong in our marriage. So did he. Sometimes what we thought was the right thing wasn't. There were words when there should have been silence; and there was silence when someone should have spoken.

One thing became clear: we had both forgotten to *live* our lives! We were so focused on the business and the details of it and life in general, that we forgot to take an occasional break, sit back, and look at the big picture. It turned out that we were better partners in business than we were in marriage.

I realized too late that what I was missing in my marriage wasn't a sense of personal and financial security, it was passion and love.

In detail, this is what happened.

~Is "Give the Best You Can" A True Statement?~

Life had taught me how to be an independent woman, fearless of any obstacles before me. To me, taking control of situations seemed an easy task and finding solutions became part of my life. Sometimes I come off as abrasive, yet I believe that being that way and my positive attitude was an inspiration for others and helping them was my greatest reward. But, of course, before you can truly help others you have to help yourself.

As soon as we got married and had our first house, I began using my business sense to save dollars and cents so that we could reach our goals faster. Rather than hiring help when my husband wasn't around, I found myself doing most chores around the house, exactly the ones my mom said not to do.

"Xiomara" she would say, "Don't lift heavy items anymore! What you're doing is a man's job, *Mi Hija*! You don't have the physical strength to do it. You'll hurt yourself! Let him do it for you. He's the man of the house. Xiomara, listen to your Mother—you're going to hurt youself!"

I did landscaping, shoveling dirt, mulch, and gravel. I planted coconut palms and other trees and plants, with a pick and shovel. I helped paint both the exterior and interior of the house. And I did other handyman-type work.

My husband would laugh at me, working like a contractor but dressed like I was going to a party. "You are always dressed up and with makeup," he would say, "But your hands! Look at the calluses!" It was quite a sight. But it didn't bother me. All I wanted was to have our house be pretty and for us to enjoy it in particular and life in general.

I was spending more money on home decor items than personal items like trendy clothes or shoes. I just felt that it was worth it, to spend the money on something that we could both enjoy. But my friends said that was a mistake; that I should spend something on myself, and give myself the credit for all I had done—I deserved it!

Money to me was never an issue, in the sense that I spend money on things I like without noting the importance of brands or how exclusive the items might be. An item at the dollar store might appeal to me more than something at a fancy galleria.

I did it to have a wonderful home for myself, my mother, and especially my husband. He was paying most of my college expenses and I was doing this to help pay him back. He was there for me, in many other ways, when I needed help. Indeed, we helped one another and I was grateful for him and proud of him.

However, I confused the feeling of being grateful with the reality of married life. I soon found myself feeling that I had to do these duties, since it was a wifely duty within a marriage, and to give him the space he needed to work and relax. [My, how times have changed!]

All I wanted was for him to shine. I felt it was my duty was to always encourage him to move forward. "You need to move out of the company you are working for now. You need to open your own business. You are capable and smart. You can do it! I'm here for you all the way," I told him, forgetting a little about myself.

We began a small business and invested our time and money in its startup and growth. I knew that for it to be a success, it had to be our primary focus. We had to lose ourselves in the business. However, I didn't realize that we would lose our selves in the business. It took a while but eventually it became a success.

My husband was also doing well at his regular job and we began to put money aside. But along with the money, our time together was being put aside as well.

"Things are fine," he would remind me. "Everything's going to plan. Don't worry, I'm working hard so I can retire early and we can enjoy everything we've made."

I had college, and the attendant homework. We had our own business. And on weekends he brought paperwork home with him. We hardly ever took a vacation, and if we did, he would take paperwork with him. At first, I was happy that he was so committed to our plan. However, as a year passed, I began to feel as though our relationship was lost amongst the pages of paperwork.

I tried, but couldn't talk to my mother about how I felt. I prayed but couldn't hear a clear answer. And when my husband talked, he talked money and finances. He talked about a bright financial future. Maybe it was jealousy, or I was hearing though the ears of loneliness, but I began to wonder if he was talking about our future or his own? Was my feeling that our personal relationship was slipping by shaping how I viewed things? Maybe seeing things that weren't really there?

I did the research and persuaded my husband to start investing some of our monies in real estate. The real estate supply was higher than the demand and it was a buyer's market. It was time to buy and sell, flip those houses, to generate income, and we did.

Now we had our small business, our real estate business, my remaining college, business meetings with clients and bankers, and only occasionally time for friends. Never, it seemed, time for ourselves.

But we were both dedicated to our success, so it was all right. Wasn't it? After all, everything I was learning while attending F.I.U. I was applying to our day-to-day business operations. From a single strategy to expand our business, to the use of sophisticated legal nomenclature that could help me deal with the company's business contracts. My major was in Business, specializing in Marketing. I knew that this was the perfect combination for achieving business success. True enough. It just wasn't right for achieving marital success.

The idea of a separation was already crossing my mind. So too was a sense of guilt. I felt responsible for encouraging him to open the business. I felt responsible for helping turn the marriage into a business transaction.

And now that the business was growing, I was thinking about leaving him?

But, the more I thought about it, the more I realized that I right. Sure, I shared responsibility, but it was not my fault. After all, he involved me in his way of living life. And I worked hard doing what I had to as well as protecting him.

I looked up to him, looked after him, and protected him as though he was a child. I didn't allow anyone to hurt him or take advantage of him in business or life. He had nothing to worry about, not with me there. I would go to the market and take the food to the office, so he didn't have to leave his office. I would make him breakfast on weekend mornings and take it to his desk, so he didn't even have to leave the home office. Everything was for his comfort and success. The only thing I didn't do…was look after myself. Where was *I* in all of this?

As I took care of him, I was still doing my job. Maybe I was right to think about my own future, about my own happiness, but I was still a partner in our enterprises and I owed it to the both of us to continue. After all, I would money myself.

I reviewed financial statements, made changes to reduce cost and increase profits, promoted our business wherever and whenever possible. The company was growing, and growing to the extent that it was hard to keep up. There was no time to turn back—I just couldn't leave now. Love, passion, and business seemed a heady cocktail, but as I became drunk with success, I realized the sobering hangover of despair came with an emotional cost. It seemed that being unhappy was just my destiny.

~To Love and Loss~

Did he feel as I did? Or was he still drunk on success? Could he see—or was he simply ignoring—the full picture in our relationship?

These and a thousand nagging questions and doubts pestered me waking and sleeping. The circumstances were different, but the stress was just as bad as I felt with my abusive father. And stress, whatever the cause, destroys things, makes them fall apart.

Worry, long hours, lack of good sleep, bad diet, and more contributed to a health crisis. My health always been precarious, with orthodonture problems from my accident, and my heart arrhythmia. Now I had developed lymphatic nodules on the left side of my neck that would have to be removed surgically.

I told my husband what the doctor had told me. He was concerned, but somewhat distant. No "Oh, my God!" outburst of emotion, rather a casual concern. "How bad will it be?" he asked. "How long will it take to recover?" Perhaps, I thought, he did care in some unimpassioned way.

"Will you okay in time for the bankers meeting on the fifteenth?"

And there it was. Did he care more about the business than my health after all these years?

Money is not the root of evil. It's LOVE of money that is the root of evil. So, since we had money—what if we had something else to love? Someone else to love?

After almost seven years of marriage, we finally decided to have children. We needed a change in our lives. It was not because a child was going to keep us together, but rather that something, maybe a laugh or a kiss from our child, would fill our lives with the happiness we couldn't find elsewhere.

I was thrilled to learn I was pregnant! After years of wishing and trying, it happened. But due to my health problems, it was a high-risk pregnancy.

We were excited, and scared. Being parents wouldn't come easy for me. I carried deep emotions from my childhood. But I swore to the Almighty that I would provide a loving environment for my child. He or she would *NEVER* go through what I went through. Both of us would love this child, even if we no longer quite loved each other.

I followed my doctor's orders to the tee. I took care of myself. I was cautious about walking, how I moved; I monitored my heart rate and never allowed myself to become angry or upset and risk a rise in my blood pressure. I stayed in bed as much as possible.

But eight weeks into the pregnancy I realized I was bleeding. I called out to my mom, crying, "I'm bleeding! I am bleeding, Mimi! What should I do?"

"Call the doctor immediately," she hollered back, coming to my aid. "How did it happen and when did you start bleeding?"

"I went to the kitchen to make my lunch and I felt something running down my legs."

"I'm so cold and shivering. I'm not only bleeding, I'm think I'm having contractions, too," I cried. "Oh, God!" I silently screamed, as much in pain and anger as in prayer.

Within minutes, I was in the emergency room. "You're having a miscarriage, Xiomara," the doctor said.

I wept. A thousand thoughts ran helter-skelter through my mind. I believe in destiny and how God works in mysterious ways, so was having a child not a part our destiny? Was this part of His plan? Was it because my husband and I were successful? Was it that we already had enough? And why didn't I listen to my mother when she told me, "Don't lift heavy furniture, don't do a man's job?" Or maybe, it was because I had used contraceptives for too long; to avoid having children so that we could have a profitable business? My husband arrived and we went home. Both of us silent and tearful.

Neither of us spoke much for the next several days, my mother taking care of my needs as my husband continued to go to work. I tried to fault him for it, but his lack of concern and going to work was simply how he coped with the tragedy.

For myself, I coped in a different manner. I came to accept that there was only one answer. God knows His plans. I don't. I play the hand God deals, and pray for guidance to do what's right. I have to accept that His timing is perfect, even if I don't think it is. I knew I must, once again, look for the light in the darkness.

A few months later, after a physical and emotional recovery, I filed for divorce. It wasn't an easy decision but it was best for the both of us.

Sure, to many we looked like the perfect couple, in love, and with money. So how could this happen? "Seriously you're getting a divorce? But now, after all, you worked for? Now? When the company is doing so well? Are you crazy? Why would you leave him," I was asked a million times by family and friends.

A few were concerned for me, but most simply wondered about the business. I couldn't believe what I was hearing. Didn't they realize that money couldn't replace happiness? Didn't they see that it was a very poor substitute for honest emotion and love? Couldn't they understand that business can become so addictive that you give up everything and sacrifice anyone to be successful?

They couldn't and didn't. At first.

As the separation and divorce became more real to them, most of my family and friends began to understand what I had gone through and why I had to let that life go. A few took a look at their own lives and relationships with others and money and came away with a different perspective. Without realizing it, I was fulfilling my mission; I was teaching them a lesson without even noticing it.

* * * * *

During my first marriage, there was personal and professional growth for the both of us, accomplishments and disappointments. We each made choices that, in retrospect, were — what's the word I'm looking for, oh yeah—stupid. Yet, I've sometimes wondered, "*Should I have given our marriage another chance?*"

The answer is "no." And besides, the past is the past and all I and anyone else can do is learn from it and make a better future.

Indeed, we both learned our lessons. To me, my first marriage was never a failure as such, it was fourteen years of a life experience. I learned to grow as both an individual and as a professional woman, and that empowers me to this day. I also learned to let go of preconceptions and animosity. Moreover, I learned the importance of acceptance and forgiveness. So now, if anyone asks me to describe my former husband, I would say, "My Rock." That was what he was. The something solid and strong in my young womanhood, as I was attempting to find myself and my way in life. And, despite everything, I am thankful for him. I accept my fourteen years with him as one of God's "mysterious ways, His wonders to perform."

Today my former husband continues to run the company and is happily remarried with children. And I...

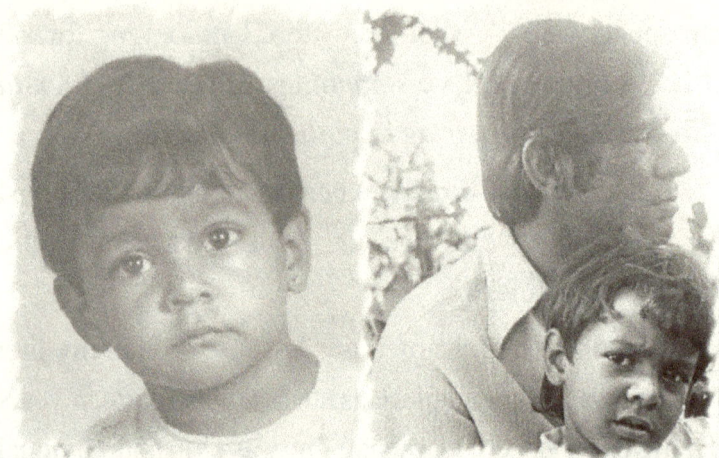

MOM, DAD, SISTER, AND I. MY FIRST MODELING
EXPERIENCE.

TRANSITIONS IN LIFE. "A WOMAN ON A MISSION" —
THAT BECAME MY PERSONAL SLOGAN.

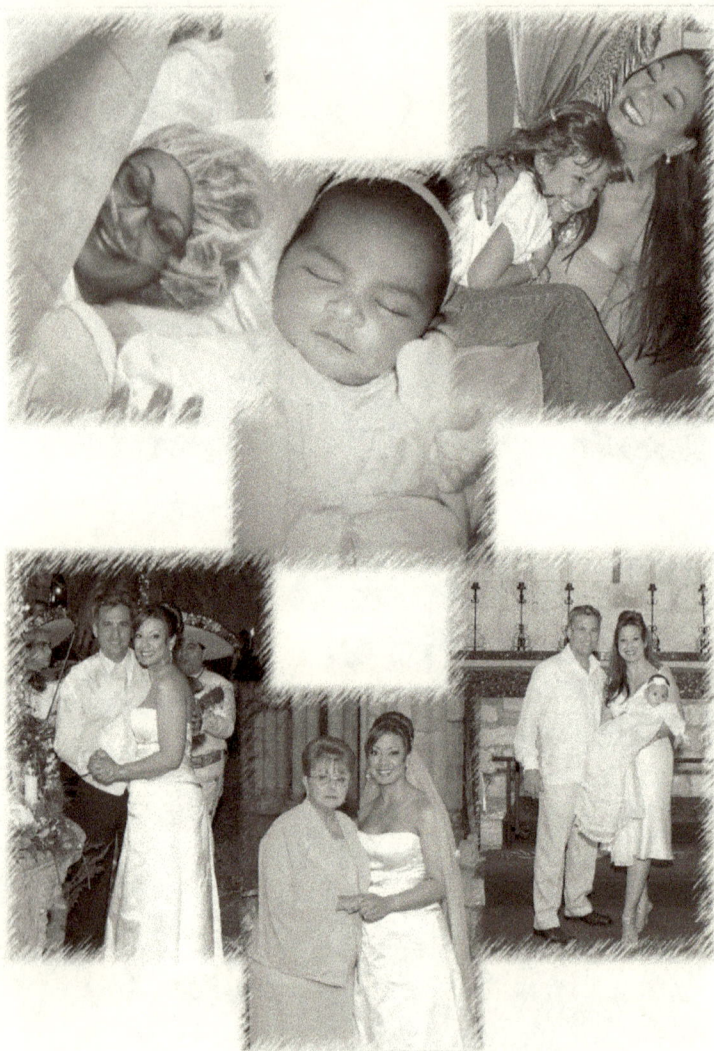

MY DAUGHTER WAS BORN. MY SECOND MARRIAGE.
MY MOM AND I. MY DAUGHTER'S BAPTISM.

MY MOM, SISTER AND I, SEVERAL MONTHS BEFORE
SHE WENT TO HEAVEN. ME WEARING A WIG TO
MAKE MY MOM SMILE AS SHE WAS WEARING
HER OWN.

PUBLIC FIGURES THAT INSPIRED ME THROUGHOUT
THIS JOURNEY. PAT RILEY. GLORIA ESTEFAN, GISELLE
BLONDET. ISMAEL CALA. MARIO KREUTZBERGER.

RECORDING FOR MY SHOW. NINO PERNETTI'S CAFFÉ
ABBRACCI. MANDARIN ORIENTAL, MIAMI, AND SPA.
MY HUSBAND & I. MY DECORATING SEGMENT,
MAYELA ROSALES, D'LATINOS AL DIA TV SHOW.

BEHIND THE SCENES, "EL SHOW DE XIOMARA
MARTINEZ" AND MY GREAT TEAM, LAUNCHED ON
TELEMUNDO AND UNIVISION SOUTHWEST FLORIDA.

MY MIRACLE, ANGEL, AND INSPIRATION IN LIFE, MY
DAUGHTER KASSANDRA. BORN SEPTEMBER, 2005 AT
1:30 PM, MIAMI. 8-1/2 POUNDS AND 19 INCHES.

MAKING MY HIGH SCHOOL PROUD. INSPIRING UNIVERSITY STUDENTS AFTER CHIME NETWORK WAS DEVELOPED.

CHAPTER 11

A GLIMPSE OF LIGHT

Going out with my friends after my divorce was both therapeutic and a bit of a dream come true. I purchased an apartment at the beach, a new sports car, and I began to travel. It was time to reward myself and finally enjoy everything I had worked for. Besides, I saw it as fit compensation.

I was thirty-five years old, brimming with plans and hopes. I was open to anything, since I was never certain what God had in store for me. I was thankful for what God had given me and I prayed a simple prayer for happiness.

I dated for a while trying to find the right person with whom to build a relationship. It was fun at first, but nothing—and no one—seemed right. I was simply not ready for a new relationship.

I had a support base of personal and business friends and acquaintances, so I was never lonely. There was always dinners, small parties, movies, business events—something to keep me occupied. Plus, I always had people with whom I could just relax and reminiscence.

One of these people was a fellow student I had met at Miami Dade Community College, who became a study partner and friend. Paul had often come to the house to study or help me with projects when I needed an extra set of hands. He was personable and friendly, and earned my then husbands trust and respect.

We phoned each other frequently, and although it was mainly about classes, the conversation would usually lead to other things that were going on in our lives. Over time, we learned that we could talk to each other about anything. It was nice to have a male friend who had no expectations other than friendship.

He knew what was going on in my life and I learned what was happening in his. I had trouble in my marriage; he was starting a relationship. I was thinking about divorce; his brother was going through one—he could sympathize. Eventually, Paul and I finally graduated from

Florida International University and our goals were accomplished. As we continued our friendship and we had the same interest in real estate; he had just passed his real estate exam, he made my business in real estate easier to negotiate. Literally. Paul was my agent for several transactions. I was always grateful for his professional (and personal) advice.

"I meant for you and my brother to meet for a long time, "he said, "but you two were always off track. When you were dating someone, he was not and vice versa. But, now that you're both single..."

I smiled politely and said, "Thank you, but I don't want to date anyone; especially if he's your brother." As soon as I said it, I knew that it had come out wrong.

"No, that's not what I meant," I said and reached out and grabbed his elbow. "It's just that I don't want any conflict of interest. I don't want to lose our friendship. You know how dating your brother could change things between us." He nodded but didn't look convinced.

"Look," I said in an attempt to make amends, "I appreciate your concern for me and your brother, so if you want to, let's get together next week. We'll have dinner to celebrate our last real estate acquisition. But that's it. Okay?"

"Sounds good," he said. "Sorry for the presumption; it's just that I always thought you two would hit it off."

I gave him a hug and whispered, "Thank you for caring."

Friday night my doorbell rang and inside me, there was a butterfly feeling which I had not expected. I was nervous about the evening. Everything felt a little awkward.

"Nice to meet you! Enjoy yourselves," I said and began to turn away to see my friend and his wife. Paul lightly grabbed my elbow as his brother and wife drifted toward the drink table.

His face was lightly tanned and his temples slightly grayed; he looked a little older than me. I vaguely remembered that he was a policeman, divorced, and …that was about it.

The four of us were exceptionally polite the entire evening. "I hope everything is all right," I said.

"Everything looks and smells great!" Paul said, his wife smiling in agreement.

The rest of the evening was casual conversation and a few drinks. Each of us came to open up a little and the awkwardness I had first felt began to ebb. Felix was quite charming. And he had the most piercing eyes.

I discovered that we had both been through a tough divorce.. He was a police officer. Though it had been only a few hours, I was feeling relaxed in Felix's company. It was a comfortable feeling I hadn't experienced in quite a while. Was this part of God's plan for me? I couldn't tell, but what was obvious to me was that I was becoming attracted to this man. And I didn't fight the feeling.

From that day on, we arranged our schedules to meet as often as possible. Soon it was daily. There was always something new and exciting to do or talk about. We walked, talked, dined, did "touristy" stuff—anything to spend time together. We were old enough to know better, but we acted like teenagers.

There was so much to learn about each other. We each found it easy to "open up" about things we would otherwise keep secret. Things moved rather quickly but it all seemed so natural. It all seemed so right. I was happy.

~A Fairy Tale Wedding~

The fairy tale began and I found myself doing everything that a bride dreams of—something that I never did in my first marriage. I was still living my dream. At first, we decided to have a small, intimate wedding. However, it is the bride's prerogative to change her mind, so I did.

We chose a wonderful venue for the wedding, St. Bernard de Clairvaux church, known as The Spanish Monastery. It is a real medieval Spanish monastery cloister brought over stone by stone by newspaper tycoon William Randoph Hearst in 1924, during one of his European antiques buying sprees. Luckily, it never made it to his property in California, so this princess could marry in a medieval "castle."

Everything seemed magical: going to food tastings to select just the right entrée and wedding cake; trying on wedding gowns; selecting the right colors and flowers for the décor and my bridal bouquet; and eating at restaurants with my handsome fiancée while we planned every detail of the wedding. It was going to be the wedding I had always dreamed of.

Since it was my second wedding, I selected a simple silk champagne wedding dress and chose a soft Spanish-style veil with a beautiful design of gold crystals on the bottom. If I was going to be princess on my wedding day, I might as well look the part!

As we were getting married in February, Valentine's month, I decided that my bouquet would be a round red flower arrangement.

We decorated The Spanish Monastery like a palace and the ambiance was magical. Valentine's red with accents of gold and cream colored the décor and tables. The table settings themselves were understated but elegant.

The beautiful buffet was lit in such a way as to highlight its placement in the Monastery's cloisters. There were two ice sculptures shaped like doves, each engraved with our initials, reflecting both the ambient lighting and our special union.

In the center of the cloister, there was a closed antique water-well decorated with red and beige-colored flowers. The wedding cakes fondant was a light cream color decorated with fondant roses, offset by fresh red flowers around the cakes base, which added an extra touch of glamour.

The wedding planning had been trying, but it was worth it now that the day had arrived. I was nervous, but not reluctant. After all, it seemed that my prayers had been answered.

CHAPTER 12

MY ANGEL,
A MIRACLE FROM GOD

y husband and I were so excited because
we were going to be parents. The little
"plus sign" on the stick meant the world to
us. I felt blessed and thankful to God for this gift:
having a child when I wanted one most. It was the
answer to my last unanswered prayer. "I probably did
something right during my life to receive this
extraordinary blessing," I thought.

"Xiomara, why don't you come with me? The
Doctor is waiting for you in her office," the nurse said.
I instinctually knew something wasn't right, but tried to

stay positive. I asked the nurse, "Is everything ok?" but she didn't answer. The hall seemed longer than I remembered and grew longer with every step I took and every thought that raced through my mind.

The nurse knocked softly on the office door and then opened it, holding it for me to walk through. The doctor stood up from her chair and gestured to the chair on the other side of her desk.

"Why don't you take a seat, Xiomara," she said. "I have your blood test results."

I raised my eyebrows and had a "So?" look on my face. The stick said I was pregnant and my visit to her was simply to confirm that and to see what steps I needed to take to protect myself and my pregnancy. I knew I had to be careful because of my heart, so what was this about?

"Your hormone levels are too high," she said.

"Ok…" I said, that "So?" look still on my face. "What does that mean?"

She leaned over her desk and I instinctively leaned towards her.

"It means, Xiomara, that your ovaries are not functioning."

I tried to understand what she was saying.

"There is nothing you can do if your ovaries are not working, Xiomara. I'm sorry to have to tell you that you're unable to have children."

I sat there staring at her. I just looked at her. There were no tears, no words; just a simple Mona Lisa smile to demonstrate that I was in control of my emotions. After a few seconds I asked, "But what about the test?"

"It was a false positive. That happens sometimes."

I kept my smile as I sat back in my chair.

The doctor still leaned forward over her desk and smiled a little herself.

"I know how this must feel, Xiomara," and she probably did as I'm certain she had to tell patients this before, but there is some good news. All isn't lost. You could still bear children, but you'll need to get an egg donor, maybe someone you know, your sister for instance, or you could go through a donor bank."

I inadvertently nodded my head. The doctor sat back in her chair, reached for a business card she had on the desktop and began to hand it to me.

"I would like to give you a phone number-it's for an acupuncturist. I want her to help you with the bone density and hormone issues. I know that acupuncture is still considered alternative medicine by some, but it often works for my patients, so you never know. In fact, I had a fifty-seven years old patient that had already entered menopause and became pregnant because of the acupuncture sessions. Like I said, you never know."

I took the card and glanced at it, but didn't really see anything. My mind was numb and everything was done by instinct and rote.

"Thank you for everything, doctor," I said reaching out my hand to shake hers and quickly leaving the office.

I don't remember walking to my car, but there I was. I sat in it for several minutes going over everything the doctor told me; trying to absorb it all. Suddenly I found myself hyperventilating and I tried to control my breathing but I couldn't. I placed my arms and head on the steering wheel and broke down in tears.

I'm not sure how I made it home safely, but when I got there I threw myself on my bed and continued to cry. The phone rang but I ignored it. I'm sure it was my mother or husband asking how my visit went, and I was in no mood to talk to them about it. I still couldn't believe it all and I needed time to work my way through all of this.

I needed to try and understand why this was suddenly happening. I had already been through so much in my life, it didn't seem fair. I needed to have a deep conversation with God.

My daily walk along the beach became sit down meditation. I sat on the warm afternoon sand on the beach near our house, my toes just touching the Gulf water lapping the shore, closed my eyes and prayed.

The bright noon sunlight came through my eyelids, so instead of a dark world before me I saw a red one. My emotions rose as I believed it not to be blood red but rather the reddish glow of the setting sun. I chose to understand the color as indicating the close of a long day and the rise of a peaceful night followed by a new day; one filled with hope.

I prayed, "You know and *only* You know why, what, and where my life should be heading. I pray that You just give me strength and show me the light, open my eyes so I can see my path and open my ears so I can hear You clearly."

I leaned forward, raised my knees to my chest, clasped my hands in prayer and emptied my mind, hoping to hear Him.

The first thing that entered my mind was thoughts about my former husband and the life we led. I still harbored a small sense of guilt about the breakup of our marriage. But I knew that I had to get on with my life, move forward from the past, and so I did.

Next came memories of my father. The kind man and the scoundrel. My *Papi* and his evil twin. I realized that my ex and my current husband were really father-figures, because I had never had a *real* father. My mother had taken on those duties, and—bless her—did what she could, but it was no substitute. I understood that while both of my husbands certainly filled a part of that void, I had only one, true father. "You are my Father and my only Father," I thought, acknowledging God. That simple realization became the philosophy of my life.

I understood right there and then, that it we had a beautiful connection. That what I needed wasn't necessarily what I wanted, and that—even though I often didn't recognize it at the time—God always provided what I truly needed. So, though I had been blessed with financial success, I knew in my heart that money was only a means to an end. I had to use it wisely to help myself so that I could spread the word, show the hope and miracles that I had so far found in my life. I had God's blessing to learn from my human frailty and the mistakes I had made. I believe that learning makes me stronger and by making me stronger, He uses me to inspire and touch peoples' lives. Though I had certainly suffered, others had been burdened with more pain than I had, so I felt humbled by the lesser pain I had to endure. Perhaps, good arises from pain. After all, without any of my experiences, I wouldn't be able to comprehend the suffering of others. So, did I really need a child now? Was this the right moment. I *wanted* a child but I need a child? Oh, God, what now?

I was in a meditative state, but felt the suns warmth on my skin, the cool water that was rising at the shore, the sounds of people splashing the water as they walked between the water and me. I was both within and without the world at that moment. I was scared, angry, frustrated with my lot, myself, and God—yet still I felt calm, relaxed, grateful for everything, and one with the Almighty. I had found in my faith a father in whom I could finally trust, a father who would give me both strength and unconditional love; a father who would see me through this.

I returned home and avoided my mother's phone calls, and told Felix that I didn't feel well and needed quiet and bed rest. At breakfast the next day, I calmly explained to my family what the doctor had said.

My husband and mother were shocked. They were surprised at what the doctor said, but more so at my calm demeanor. "You don't seem too worried about this," my husband said, wondering if I was okay with the news.

"I know everything will work out for the best," I said, just as my mother reached across and took my hand in hers. She had tears streaming down her cheeks.

"Mimi, trust me," I said to calm her fears, "It will all be fine. Trust in me because I trust in the Lord."

She nodded, let go of my hand, rose from her chair, kissed the top of my head and walked to the door. She was so emotional that she couldn't look at me, but said as she walked away, "Anything you need, Niña…anything at all…"

Felix took out his mobile phone. "I'm calling off today, honey. You need me here." It was a sweet gesture.

"Thank you," I said. "But really, I need to be alone for a while. You go to work. It'll take your mind off everything."

"But…" he began to protest.

"Go! It'll be all right. Like I told Mimi—trust me!"

He shook his head and put his phone back in his pocket. "You're something else!" he said, kissed me on the forehead and started to get ready for work.

I have always been a problem-solver. As much as the news about my condition hurt me, I decided to try to turn the situation around. With the house empty, I took out the card the doctor had given me and called the acupuncturist.

I then began doing research online about my condition. I looked at dozens of articles in medical journals (some of which I actually understood!) as well as research on popular medical sites. Many of the articles seemed contradictory and made for dire reading. Others offered hope. A few suggested that there might be a way to re-stimulate my ovaries and get them to produce eggs again through some techniques in In Vitro Fertilization (IVF).

In vitro fertilization is the most effective type of assisted reproductive technology to help a woman become pregnant. I looked up clinics near me and found one about a three-hour drive away. I called my doctor to ask about them and though she said that she could recommend them, she cautioned that I shouldn't hold out too much hope. I thanked her for her advice, but I knew that I could hold out hope because I was held in God's hands.

The three-hour drive seemed much longer than that when I made my first visit to the IVF clinic. Everyone was exceptionally kind and explained the process I'd undergo. I was asked to fill out an exhaustive questionnaire and list any known medical problems that might affect my treatment. I listed my heart problems and the low progesterone levels that run in my family. Today they would begin initial blood work to determine when I would ovulate and to check my hormone levels. The actual procedure only took a few minutes and I was told that they would call me with the results.

I had already begun my acupuncture treatments with the super thin needles and herbal teas uncertain of what to expect. My doctor indicated that thousands of years of Chinese medicine made such practices a possibly helpful procedure for me; just don't get my hopes up. She didn't realize that I had more than hope, I had faith. Between both modern and ancient medical treatments and my belief that I was following God's plan, I knew that I'd experience a miracle. And I did. Shortly after my first acupuncture treatment, I had my period!

I returned to the IVF office on the third day after my period started, excited and happy to share my good news. The nurses were happy for me and took a second vial of blood for analysis.

The next day, the phone rang. "This is Dr. Ortiz from the IVF clinic. May I speak with Xiomara?"

"Yes," I answered tentatively. I was so afraid that there was something wrong with the blood work.

"Xiomara, your blood work is positive. It looks like you are pregnant..." I was so excited that I almost dropped the phone!

"However," the voice continued, "the Beta HCG is too low. This test checks specific levels of hormones in the body, which helps the doctor determine if a woman is pregnant, and/or how the pregnancy is going. So, while the initial signs indicate pregnancy, we are asking you not to get your hopes up. The fact that the Beta is so low means that the pregnancy is what's known as a 'chemical' pregnancy. This usually results in a very early miscarriage that usually occurs within a week after getting a period and most women don't even notice."

Again, I almost dropped the phone.

"Just rest at home, have a heating pad ready and wait until you feel a big pain. The bleeding will let you know that the chemical pregnancy is over. Come in the next day after to make sure the episode is over."

I paused, stunned.

"Xiomara?" Dr. Ortiz asked.

"Yes. Thank you, doctor." I said robotically, and ended the call. I felt weak from the news and plopped into a chair and cried.

The drive for my third visit to the clinic felt longer than ever. My mood had changed from depression to defiance and I had a thousand questions to ask. *"What is "chemical" pregnancy again?" "How do I increase my Beta HCG levels?" "Is that connected to my low progesterone?"*

The doctor was kind and understanding. He had obviously dealt with confused and belligerent patients before. I kept emphasizing, "Please consider that my progesterone levels are always very low. It's a family thing."

"That might be, Xiomara, but progesterone levels have nothing to do with Beta levels. Progesterone is a female hormone produced during the release of mature eggs from an ovary. This hormone helps prepare the lining of the uterus and, well, I don't like to use progesterone for a pregnancy. Our philosophy is that if we need to use anything to maintain a pregnancy, then it is not viable. Let's let time take its' course," the doctor told me.

"And another thing," he added, "I know you told me that you are going to an acupuncturist and you are taking some herbs. I need you to stop taking the herbs because their chemicals will confuse the hormone level results."

I listened intently and nodded my head.

"Thank you, doctor," I said. He made a lot of sense and he knew best. But, I decided that if the herbal pills brought about my period the first time, then I would take my chances and continue with both treatments at the same time. I felt that I had to risk it all. I didn't feel that I had many options—or time—left. I was in my thirties and if I wasn't producing eggs nor menstruating, all I could hope for was the second period, and go from there. I had nothing to lose.

I only told my husband that the visit went well and he was encouraged about everything, and that we should keep trying.

The following month I decided not to lose a minute of time when my possible period approached. I bought as many ovulation sticks as possible to cover the entire ovulation cycle. We'd try; I'd check. We'd try again; I'd check.

Was I correct? Yes, indeed, I got a positive result! But the day I had minor spotting.

According to the clinic, for them to see any type of hormone levels, I had to wait three days after having a *full* flow of blood, and they didn't consider spotting as a regular flow. However, being anxious (and a pain in the butt) I called the doctor and requested to have one done regardless. They agreed, reluctantly. A few days later, my phone rang.

Having already had an issue with the chemical pregnancy, I was expecting to hear that that was what it was. They would let me know about my blood test results, but for now they recommended that I contact my obstetrician and have a vaginal ultrasound to rule out the possibility of an ovarian cyst. Again, I almost dropped the phone.

An ovarian cyst? What? Could it be? Why?

After turning to God and praying, I called my mother.

"Oh my God, Mimi, it I might have an ovarian cyst! That's what the doctor told me."

"Forget about that, Xiomara. You don't have any cyst! That doctor has no idea what he's talking about," my mother said to encourage me; but I could hear the worry in her voice.

We said a little prayer together and we ended the call. I then called my OBGYN to schedule the ultrasound.

After I hung up the phone I realized that I had been so caught off guard by the phone call from the clinic that I hadn't really understood that the doctor did NOT tell me that I HAD an ovarian cyst, just that that might be a possibility and the ultrasound would determine my condition. I'd like to think that an angel whispered that to me to keep me calm.

Life being chaos, my unexpected visit to my OBGYN was scheduled in the morning of the same day we were leaving to visit Disney World to join other family members for a mini-vacation. I was packing when my phone rang and I hurriedly answered assuming that it was some cousin calling about the trip.

"Xiomara? This is the clinic. Your results are positive again. Please make sure you do the same steps as last month. Use the heating pad and just wait. Unfortunately, your Beta counts are too low again."

After a curt thank you and goodbye, I called my obstetrician to cancel my ultrasound. I'd be charged for the visit as it was only a few hours before the appointment, but what mattered to me was that I had positive results. I finished packing, picked up my purse and heating pad, and went to Disney World as I planned.

Everyone got together and planned their day—rides, where to eat-the usual things. However, Felix and I knew that we had to stay at the hotel to avoid walking and possibly having a miscarriage. No one knew the real reason why it was that we didn't enter the park. We were just too tired and needed a relaxing few days alone, we said. After all, we'd see everyone at dinner.

That night, I went to bed, placed my heating pad next to the night table and waited and waited. Nothing was happening and I fell asleep.

The next morning, I saw a big pink line in the shape of a circle underneath me on the towel I had placed there. I felt no bleeding or pain. Worried, we made the excuse that something had come up and my husband and I had to get back home.

We drove straight to the IVF clinic where they took blood and I asked them to please rush the test results. My husband and I waited anxiously over the next three hours until my nurse called us over.

"Neither the lab or Doctor Ortiz can explain this," she began, and my heart sank.

"But it seems that the Beta levels are rising! Everyone is so confused! But, that's good news for you, Xiomara!"

Felix hugged my shoulder and kissed me on the forehead as we walked to the car. I was elated at the prospect and understood why the clinic had been confused—they didn't expect God to work the miracle He had.

As soon as we got home, I called my obstetrician, apologized again for cancelling my ultrasound and asked her to place me on the progesterone treatment.

I had to convince her that this was what I truly wanted after she explained the possible risks. She was cautious and explained that it might be a little early to start the treatment. Also that I should let my IVF doctor know about the treatment, after all, he'd see it in the blood tests. Lastly, that the progesterone pills she would prescribe were fast, efficient, and guaranteed to screw up my hormones—"Be prepared for the ride, because the hormones are gonna drive you crazy!" and then laughed and added, "And your poor husband too!"

There were risks but none that I was unwilling to take. I felt that it was God and His angels guiding me. I believed that it this miracle was because of my faith and belief and I needed to express that now.

* * * * *

For the next eight weeks, the IVF Company monitored my pregnancy. It became obvious that I was taking progesterone, but it seemed to have a positive effect. But even with that the probability that I might go through the entire pregnancy was very low.

My first ultrasound didn't show anything important, according to Dr. Ortiz. He took several photos of the screen that I asked to see it but was told, "We don't like to give high hopes to our patients." I didn't argue but was a little upset.

My second ultrasound was schedule on February 14, Valentine's Day, just a coincidence as it was the only day the clinic had available—but it was a wonderful coincidence.

As I lay on the table, having cold gel rubbed on my abdomen, staring up at a monitor as the technician began to run the icy paddle over me, I was uncertain exactly what it was I was looking at. I closed my eyes for a few seconds and prayed that when I opened them I would see a miracle.

"Just there, doctor," the tech said as Dr. Ortiz stepped in and took over the paddle.

"Look at that, Xiomara," he said. "See that little button, kind of the size of a wedding ring?"

I did see it. But what does it mean? I finally heard the words I desperately wanted to hear.

"Well, young lady, that is your son or daughter! You've got a normal, regular pregnancy! Time to say 'goodbye' to me and 'hello' to your obstetrician!"

I looked at that tiny thing on screen and cried. I still have the copy of the ultrasound photo of my little miracle and I still cry whenever I look at it.

* * * * *

My little miracle was born weighing eight and a half pounds and measuring nineteen inches. Wrinkled skin, eyes closed tight and white goo on her tiny face, she was the most beautiful thing I had ever seen. I named her Kassandra, because I think that it is a beautiful name and because of its meaning as a prophet whose words will not be believed. That was the curse placed on the ancient Trojan Kassandra and a curse that I knew my Kassandra would break.

Indeed, as she has grown, I have seen my daughter change people's lives with her miracle story. Her kindness and loving heart captures the attention of friends, teachers, and everyone around her. Watching my daughter grow-up with integrity, honesty, humbleness, and compassion for others is an inspiration to me. Her words of hope are believed. I know that God is already using her for His Glory. Every day of my life, with her by my side, all darkness turns into light.

CHAPTER 13

A SEPARATE STRENGTH: LOVE, LOSS, AND LOVE AGAIN

"I take you, to be my wife, to have and to hold, from this day forward, for better, for worse, for richer, for poorer, in sickness and in health, until death do us part," a commitment that had given me hope, strength, spiritual security, and peace was fading away. Again.

Felix is nine years older than me. The age difference didn't matter much to either of us. We were close enough in age to have had many of the same experiences in life, shared much the same taste in music, foods, etcetera. We were part of the same generation. Moreover, we seemed to share God's blessing. But what I hadn't realized was just how much pain we also shared.

Everything was great during the "honeymoon period" of our marriage, as it should be. In fact, as this was a second marriage for the both of us we worked hard to make sure that the honeymoon lasted. We were kind and considerate of each other, recognized each other's needs, understood that sometimes we needed to be alone together—respect each other's boundaries and allow for private time.

We were mature enough to understand that we each carried emotional baggage from both our lives and previous marriages and we each had to be there for each other to help work through it. And we were there for each other. At first.

After three years, however, our pasts seemed to catch up with us. Sometimes your past can be so traumatic that its ghostly presence haunts you forever and no matter what you do to dispel that frightening spirit, it just won't leave you alone. So it was with the two of us.

Neither of us was to blame. I loved him and he loved me. We weren't caught up in business or running headlong and carelessly into our future, as I had been with my first marriage. We were mature, reasonable adults and understood that sometimes there are problems in a relationship. And too, that problems can be solved. Runaway emotions merely hinder finding a solution and reason and rationality are what is called for to reconcile any differences and resolve a problem. Still, emotions matter and sometimes explode. Sometimes a small thoughtless or inconsiderate gesture, the wrong word spoken with the wrong tone, some trivial transgression that might otherwise go without notice becomes a landmine that triggers an explosion in a relationship.

I couldn't help but wonder if we had both rushed into marriage. Had we given ourselves enough time to get to know one another? While we were old enough to know better, we treated our relationship as if we were teenagers; boundless love, couldn't wait to see each other, calling on the phone and ending conversations with "You hang up first!" "No! YOU hang up first!" and a thousand other lovey-dovey idiocies that seem so wonderful at the time but can mar an adult relationship.

And with the stress of life for us while I was getting pregnant and during my pregnancy, who could really blame him for wanting a break? We both were remorseful about what was happening to us. And I was certain that most of the blame lie with me.

"God, not again!" I cried out in my mind. It was both a prayer and a question. I seemed that both my husband and I were reliving our past. Why? What was happening? Had I mis-stepped along the path that He had laid out for me? Both Felix and I had faults, but surely God had given me eyes to see them and a heart to forgive them.

I wondered if it was my fault because I had developed such a strong character. Maybe my heart was calloused. Maybe I simply wasn't deserving of *any* mans love. Maybe my strength and self-esteem was too overbearing and had been too much for him to take. Maybe if I… Maybe if he… Maybe. *Maybe* became the first word of almost any though I had.

Felix and I decided that a separation, some time apart, was best for us. Neither felt that our differences were irreconcilable. We simply needed a break from each other. Soon I found myself alone with a three-year-old daughter.

My mother called me every night to check up on me. I appreciated her love and concern. And I appreciated her now, as an adult, much more than I had as a child. It had been hard for me to truly understand everything she had been through. How scared and lonely she must have felt, essentially raising a daughter on her own. Moreover, I appreciated the irony of my now being in her position. I was reliving her past.

Please understand that though neither I nor my daughter suffered any verbal or physical abuse, as had my mother, I was—in my mind—suffering as my mother had. I too felt lonely, desperate, and scared about raising a daughter on my own. In fact, I was only three-years-old when my parents began having problems and had a first separation. History repeated itself.

Yet, things were really quite different from what my mother had experienced. For one thing, my husband and I agreed that he would be an active part of Kassandra's life during our separation. Another was that we would stay in touch, even meet occasionally. Also, he and my mother had a great relationship—she understood him, perhaps better than I did.

I was lonely in our house with only my toddler daughter and my mother's phone calls to keep me company. Family members wanted to drop by, but I always thanked them politely and asked them to respect my privacy. Sometimes, late at night, long after my daughter was fast asleep, I would walk a few steps stare up at the shimmering stars and lose myself in the vastness of the night sky.

Sometimes too, I would stand on the back porch and tearfully ask God to explain just what was happening; why was my faith being tested? Truly, Lord, was it *me*? And if it was, why punish my daughter? And then collapse, crying, onto the chaise lounge, hoping that my sobs did not drown out the voice of God I hoped to hear.

Other times, as the lonely and cruel darkness overwhelmed me, bitterness would well up inside and I would become jealous of Felix's taking Kassandra out on a Saturday, and his always wanting to talk with her on the phone when he called me. Was he playing on her emotions as my own father had done with mine? Was he using my daughter's naivety and trust to get her to side with him, as my own father had done? Indeed, sometimes when I'd make her take her bath or go to bed, she'd tell me "Daddy doesn't make me!" Was my past repeating itself?

The nights terrified me but in the light of day, I understood my fears to be irrational. God would talk to me in His own good time and my husband was simply being a wonderful father and trying to make Kassandra's life as normal as possible.

When I told my mother about this, I could hear reluctant relief in her voice.

"I told you that once you had a child you'd see things from a different perspective! At least Kassandra isn't as defiant to you as you were to me. There is nothing wrong with what your husband is doing. No child sees any parent as perfect. I certainly wasn't a perfect parent in your eyes!" I could hear the "I told you so!" in her voice. "But remember, Xiomara, what we went through. As you got older, it was your faith that helped me keep going. You would tell me that God told you this or that and that was what kept me going. You helped me become free and a better person for it. The three of you love, and need each other. So listen to your heart. Pray; and God will guide you."

I followed my mother's advice and soon after that, I felt God's presence telling me, "Be strong! You will pass through this storm and the others to follow. Learn! Open your eyes and ears and I will show you the way!"

I felt confident. I felt relieved. I slept soundly through the night for the first time in months. I was starting to understand why I was told "Learn!" I still had some personal doubts about my strength of character, but I was beginning to learn to love myself as a child of God. I saw that the struggles of both my husband's pasts and mine led us to new possibilities to learn spiritual growth. I understood that though we may forgive ourselves for past mistakes, we should never forget them so that we not repeat them. I learned to see in my husband something that had been missing over the past few months.

That is why we made it through our separation. That is why we are together as a family and have the peaceful marriage that we both deserve. After all of that, should you ask me what one thing my husband means to me, my answer—then as now—is "Hope."

CHAPTER 14

THE BEGINNING
OF MY GLORY

In search of a new investment property, I ventured to the west coast of Florida and came across a beautiful house on Marco Island. The island is known around the world for its sandy beaches, tranquility, and natural beauty. And I was so taken with the property and its location that I decided that we should move and live there instead of placing the house on the market and "flipping" it as I usually do.

"Why do you need to move so far away?" I was asked. You have everything in Miami—your family, your friends, and the business." It seemed impulsive to others but it made perfect sense to me. It felt right to me. It was the right thing to do for my family. I felt that God was guiding me. God had something big in store for me and I needed to be aware of His will and take any opportunities gave me.

Besides, I had learned to survive under more difficult circumstances and challenges, so a move from Florida's east coast to its west coast was nothing special.

As well as making real estate investments, I came up with the idea of staging properties that were on the market so they could sell faster. Staging a house requires a keen eye, a decorator's skill, and the ability to make decisions in the face of an often hostile homeowner who doesn't understand that their favorite bright red wall color might be the reason their house was still on the market 120 days after listing.

I opened a new office in Marco Island and built my real estate and staging business using my marketing skills. I didn't know anyone in the area at first, and it was quite a process creating awareness and a business reputation. However, I knew that eventually, despite any setbacks, I'd make it.

After a few months, my business began to attract attention. Not only was I good sales woman, but the houses I staged sold faster than the average list time. Even clients who initially wondered about repainting, replanting, and storing away their daughter's two rooms worth of stuffed toys agreed that a fast sale for more than asking price was worth it.

My business was featured in newspapers and magazines, my photo often included. I was asked to write articles on staging and what it could mean to the average home seller. I was even interviewed on television.

This TV exposure caused immediate interest in my business and me as a personality. I was often referred to as a "Woman Leading by Example," "A Woman with a Mission," and other inspiring names, and one opportunity led to another.

A Spanish-language magazine called me requesting an interview. They were very interested in a successful Hispanic female. I arrived at their offices and gave, what I thought, was a good interview. It was curious, though, how several people entered the room during the interview, would stare at me and then whisper something to the woman interviewing me. She'd nod, they'd smile, and walk out of the room casting me knowing looks as they did so.

I began to feel uncomfortable and asked the interviewer what was going on. She smiled at me, assured me that everything was all right; and then told me that my smile and personality would be perfect for television. I immediately spoke up about my dream of being on television and proposed for me to create the first segment on home decoration on their show. I quickly outlined my idea for the show and halfway through the woman sat back in her chair and held up her hands. "Okay, okay!" she said with a laugh. "You got it."

As I usually do, I gave every effort and spared no expense to make the segment a success. It was a great experience. While I loved being in front of the cameras, I enjoyed working behind the scene. I wanted to know every aspect of the segment—how the cameras operated, the lighting, the sound recording, the script and direction, camera angles—you name it, I wanted to learn about it. I realized that I loved the production of a television show.

I often made a nuisance of myself and got in peoples ways and under their skins, but I explained to them and the station manager, "I know I am here for a reason. It's not a coincidence I came to Marco Island. God is going to use this for something bigger." I allowed myself to follow God's lead.

After my segment ran for almost a year, I decided that I wanted to produce a show myself. The segment was a popular part of the broadcast and I shopped the idea around. I found myself interest at SW Telemundo and SW Univision. These stations are major players and I was nervous at first but realized that if God gave me the gift to lead, the charisma to empower, the strength to survive and speak with honesty, then I was more than ready!

Although it was a learning experience and there were challenges producing and hosting my own TV show, "*El Show de Xiomara Martinez*" made it on the air. My half-hour show highlighted million dollar homes, exclusive hotels, restaurants, special events and inspirational life stories.

I made twelve shows and launched them, in two of South West Florida's most important Spanish- language television channels, SW Telemundo and SW Univision. The shows were successful and I would have loved to continue producing them, but that was not God's plan. My mother was diagnosed with cancer and my life now shifted back to Miami.

My mother had driven over and visited us every other weekend. She was there to see me on television and at the studio when I produced and hosted my first show. She had always been there for me and now I needed to be there for her.

CHAPTER 15

MY GREATEST LOSS

"We need to place the house on the market and sell it. Tourists are coming to South Florida and it's the perfect season," I told my husband. There was a sense of urgency now in all that I did.

As much as I loved the house and Marco Island, I knew it was time to let it go. I began to stage and prepare the house for sale and signed a contract with a real estate agent.

I displayed it perfectly for showings. Candles lit, the TV on, with soundscape music, fresh pastries set up with orange juice, and a magazine in the lanai area. I even displayed fishing rods on the dock, as the house was on a canal. Once I had it the way I thought a buyer would want it, I left and never returned. My husband saw to it that everything was packed up and made the move to Miami with our daughter. It took only three showings and the house sold within a week, close to the asking price, no appraisal, and a cash deal.

It was not only me; it was God making His move. His plan never fails and there is nothing we can do other than obey. He was calling me out of Marco Island and calling my mother home.

* * * * *

My mom had been diagnosed with pancreatic cancer. "Six months," the doctor told me. "Six months, at best. And, no, she doesn't know. She asked us not to tell her. So please don't tell her or anyone else." That sounded like my mother. She always lived each day as though it was her last. Knowing what she had been through, that made perfect sense.

One cannot question God's plan but you can pray for some understanding. That is what I did as I watched my mother slowly succumb to her cancer. This strong woman was now frail and eventually had to stay in hospital.

Her room was typical. There were two beds, a chair, a small sofa, and medical equipment. I stayed with her and slept on the uncomfortable small sofa. Nothing could separate me from her. She had always been with me when I needed her and leaving her alone now was unthinkable. I showered in her small bathroom. My husband brought me changes of clothes. I wiped her chin when she ate—although she always brushed my hand away, "For heaven's sake, Xiomara, I can take care of myself!" But this time, she couldn't.

* * * * *

I tried to understand why this was happening. I tried to rationalize why God, who had given me so much, would take away my foundation. Maybe I could bargain with Him. Maybe I could have him take away all I had accomplished as a professional woman in exchange for a few more years with my mother. However, that was just a grieving daughter being wishful. God doesn't bargain. God doesn't accept bribes. God understands us and knows what is best for us, even if we don't. My mother had suffered abuse, poverty, and pain. She deserved better. And what better, I realized, than to be in heaven with her Lord.

I admired my mother for so many reasons but what I saw now amazed me. Even though she knew she was going to die, she showed a positive attitude toward life. She loved to have visitors, especially Kassandra—who wasn't aware of what was going on. My mother had lost her hair to the extensive chemotherapy she was receiving and she would put on funny wigs and play around with Kassandra and Paul, my brother-in-law, who cataloged the craziness, taking photos on his cell phone.

She was always in a good mood, polite to the doctors and nurses, joking with us, and it gave me so much hope to see her like that, so brave, so strong, that I thought at times that she was going to survive. We often prayed together and her faith and love for God was so steadfast that I thought a miracle might be possible.

She sat in silence one afternoon, gently holding my hand. She looked up and me and said, "I wish I would have given you more love, Xiomara. I wish I would have been more expressive. I wish I would have spent more time with you, when it really counted. If I only knew that something like this was going to happen."

She had never been an overly expressive woman as far as hugging, touching, or kissing were concerned. Oh, when I was a very little girl sure, but as I grew up she showed her love in other ways; ways I didn't recognize or understand until I was an adult and especially after I had a daughter of my own. I smiled at her and saw a small puddle of tears in her eyes.

"You have nothing to apologize for, Mimi. Nothing at all. No amount of kisses or hugs could compare with what you have been through and suffered for me; for us."

She shook her head, let go of my hand, and pulled her blanket to her neck. "I'm a little tired now, Xiomara," she said as she closed her eyes. This was the first time I could ever remember my mother expressing any regret about anything. I bent over and kissed her cheek.

Eventually I did have to go home. Try as I might to put my life on hold, it was impossible. I was a daughter, but I also had an obligation to my husband, my business, and my own daughter. But I still spent the better part of my day at my mother's bedside.

It was heartening to see how she lived her last few months. She was in pain but never let on. If it became unbearable, she'd simply ring for the nurse; but she never said a word to anyone else with her.

Only one time did I see her cry, and that was when we gathered for prayer. One part of the prayer mentioned God's love for those we leave behind and her tears came when she realized that I was going to be alone after she was gone. Even near the end, she cared more about me than herself. It humbled me then and it still does.

"Life goes too fast and we really take it for granted," she said one evening when we cuddled in her bed. She wrapped her arms around me and I suddenly had memories of feeling this as a child. As I lay next to her, I wished time had stopped right there and then. I didn't want this feeling to go away. I felt so secure and protected in my mother's arms.

As we were hugging, I realized that I was touching the port that they placed on her for chemotherapy.

"I'm sorry Mimi, I'm hurting you." I started moving away, but she pulled me back and just held me tighter.

"It's okay," she whispered, "It's okay." Comforting me as she had always done.

~An Angel is Called Home~

The room seemed to shrink with all of us there as my family and I stood in vigil. Her nurse was there with the small portable radio she carried, tuned to a station playing Christian songs. I hoped they'd play one of my mother's favorites, so that I could see her smile one last time. The nurse had lowered the hums, clicks, and whirrs of the monitors so that my mother could listen.

I climbed onto the other bed, behind all the medical equipment and the partially closed curtain, so she could not see me. I folded my knees up to my chest, like a child in a mother's womb, and watched her through the gap. A rush of helplessness overwhelmed me. And not just helpless, I felt hopeless seeing her laying there knowing that there was nothing I could do to help her. My husband put his hand on my shoulder, but at that moment I found no comfort in anything.

She had been administered drugs to lessen her pain and her eyes were closed as she rested, saving what little strength she had left. She had felt cold and so only her face and one hand lay uncovered by the blanket. Occasionally her eyes would flutter open, glancing towards the door. I didn't know if she wanted to see someone or needed something. Then, as quickly, she'd close her eyes.

My heart was breaking. "I'm here, Mimi, I'm here," I whispered in my mind. As hard as I tried, I couldn't stop crying, and I held a pillow to my face to muffle my sobs. I wanted to jump up, hold her hand, and kiss her. It was devastating to be so powerless, knowing that what you want to do isn't the right thing to do; that a well-meaning but selfish gesture was all that it was. Yet, that was all I wanted.

I stared at her face, her eyes, her nose, the wrinkles on her brow; I looked at her small hand and her manicured nails. I knew she had only hours to live and I wanted to memorize every single detail.

* * * * *

My family entered and left the room, everyone wishing to say a last goodbye. Her life had been an open book, her struggles known to everyone in the family.

"It's time," the nurse said. "Go and be next to her." My husband helped me out of bed and I took the few steps to her bedside. This was the point of no return. The inevitable was about to happen. I couldn't save my mom.

I held her hand, it felt so light and she seemed to have no strength to grip mine. I bent down and whispered to her, trying and hoping that she could hear me. I told her how much I loved her, how much she meant to me, how much I would miss her. Through my tears I told her that all her suffering would soon be over and that she'd be heaven with her Lord. I tried to reassure her that I was going to be fine.

I remembered something that had always made her smile and I whispered, *"Madre mia! Mis ojos lindos,* you smell like gardenias, Mimi! I love how you smell!"* I wanted to make her smile one last time. *"Te Amamos, Mimi."*

The nurse watched the many silent monitors and saw that the slightly bumpy line on one was now flat. She stepped toward the bed and gestured to my husband. He gently put his hand on my shoulder and guided me away. I held onto my mother's hand as long as I could, finally letting go and watching it fall—lifeless—onto the bed.

"No!" I shouted through my sobs. I rushed back to the bed before the nurse could get there and I reached out my arms to hold my mother one last time. She was still warm, just sleeping; I lied to myself.

I moved her head towards me and held her very close in my arms. I was imagining her caressing me like she had before. I was able to hold mi *Mimi* for one last time.

"Miss, you have to go!" the nurse said as she and my husband pulled me away. I had to let go, I had to let go of my mother! And then ever so gently, ever so reluctantly, I did.

~The Red Spirit of Love~

My grandmother was forty-five years old when she gave birth to my mother, her only child. It had been a difficult delivery and a woman that age having a child was indeed a miracle. All the more so in that she was born on Saint Barbara's Day. "Her name will be Barbara," my grandmother said, "in her honor." She asked for and was given a small piece of red ribbon which she pinned to the swaddling banket. Red was the color associated with St. Barbara and my grandmother decided that her little girl would wear something red every year on her birthday-a tradition that my mother kept all her life.

On the day of her funeral instead of the traditional black, I asked everyone to wear something red to honor my mother. The women wore red dresses or a red shawl. The men had red handkerchiefs in their pockets or wore a red carnation on their lapel.

There was a trio playing the gospel sings I remembered being played in my mother's room when she passed. The casket was closed and a large arrangement of red flowers covered almost its entire length. The color red around the room represented hope, peace, and love for her and made a difference to everyone. The room was vibrant and rich, and seemed filled with the presence of the spirits of love and angels.

There was a short service after which only immediate family and my mother's closest friends were asked to stay. We opened the casket for two hours for us to say our private goodbyes.

"Mimi you look so beautiful. Your face has the perfect makeup. Your hair is the way you used to like it, and you're dressed in your favorite dress and accessories." She was wearing her glasses and they shined in the room light and gave the illusion that she was just taking a brief nap.

Everyone shared the same thoughts about her—A beautiful woman, a devoted mother, a wonderful friend, a woman who loved God, and a woman of charity. People told stories about how she kept a storage shed in her backyard and filled it with items she'd then distribute to those in need. How she was an inspiration who never took credit for what she did, but rather kept glorifying and praising God for giving her the opportunity to help others. She had suffered so much but never cried about it, choosing instead to use her misfortunes as a way to show people how to overcome their own adversities. Indeed, she was a true inspiration to me as a daughter, to my own daughter, and to everyone that knew her.

The time had come. The moment to say the final goodbye. But how could I say goodbye to my mother; your rock, your life's foundation? Oh, my dear Lord, God Almighty, help me!

My emotions overwhelmed me and I was beset by grief. My tears poured forth as uncontrolable tsunamis. I gasped for breath. And then suddenly my sobs stopped. I began to compose myself, to control my emotions. In a sudden flash of realization I saw that my own faith and love of God was my salvation. As it had been for my mother. God never fails.

I found strength in that thought and vowed to continue to do what I could to honor my mother by helping inspire others. She had always had faith in me as a guidepost for people and I would see to it that I continued to be so. I was filled with a spirit of hope and recalled that my mother had passed surrounded by loving family, listening to her favorite music, gospel, and, most importantly, listening to the two most valuable words any mother will love to hear, *"TE AMAMOS!"*

* * * * *

I believe that my mother and father are in a place where their *true* love, one that started fifty-three years ago, is now sealed forever. A place where there is no memory of hate or pain; a place of love and forgiveness. I sometimes selfishly wonder if my *Papi* ever thought of me after he left us, and as he was passing. I never forgot what he had done, but I had forgiven him and my hope is that he had forgiven himself and, in his final moments, sought God's forgiveness too.

1 Philippians 4:7 KJV "And the peace of God, which passeth all understanding, shall keep your hearts and minds through Christ Jesus."

1 John 14:18 KJV "I will not leave you comfortless: I will come to you."

CHAPTER 16

THE MYSTERY
BEHIND CHIME

What is CHIME? The name is an acronym for CHANGE – HOPE – INSPIRE – MOTIVATE – EMPOWER. Those have always been my goals; the mission I was told I would accomplish in that little white church all those years ago.

CHIME for Women with XM" (yours truly) was established to share my story, to change, give hope, inspire, motivate, and empower my audience. What started out as short segments on everything from fashion to relationship tips, from fun facts to sober accounts of abuse posted on social media began to take on a life of its own. I became an inspirational speaker and worked through, social media, or any outlet.

After my mother's passing, I asked for God's guidance and I found I felt free to express myself. I was unfettered by concern as to how some might view what had happened to my mother and me. Others certainly suffered as we had; even worse than we had. Domestic abuse, both verbal and violent physical behavior, is an inexcusable and unfortunate reality in life. Yet besides my experiences with it, I am also an example of a successful professional business woman, a possible role model at most, and an example and inspiration at least.

Surprisingly, many of the people who showed interest in CHIME turned out to be young adults, many in high school and the first years of college, who were looking for guidance as they transitioned into adulthood. So, while "CHIME for Women" continued, I created "CHIME Teaching and Learning" aimed at my other audience.

And, that is the true mystery behind CHIME. It is the mystery of God Almighty. His unfathomable way of helping us help ourselves through His allowing us to find the faith to trust Him. Letting us see that the greatest mystery in life is why we are so reluctant to do so.

~Thoughts and Reflections on CHIME Teaching and Learning~

How can we help students that sometimes fly under the radar, never go to the school counselors for help when they are in trouble or have questions? How do you help those who need help but don't seek it because of peer pressure or they way it might look to their fellow students? Students under emotional stress who might simply need someone to listen to them and give them a few words of encouragement?

When I speak to young adults I find that my most rewarding moments are when a student approaches me afterword, and then ten more join in. It's amazing to see a group develop so quickly and everyone so eager to ask questions.

Young people are screaming to be heard, desperate to talk, and eager to be motivated. They are looking for people who have gone through their same life experiences. I can relate.

During my High School years, besides being in an environment of domestic violence, my family was poor and we had few low resources. High school was difficult enough, but being a teenager added to everything else I had to bear. Plainly put, while my particular set of experiences might not be the same as theirs, I share with them the same anxieties, worries, and questions about the unknown that lies ahead of them. As I said, I can relate to them. More importantly, they can relate to me.

And it's not just high school students.

The transition from college to the workforce is a concern. What happens to college graduates that are expecting to have a job right after they graduate? Many can't find jobs related to their degree—or any job for that matter—and become depressed and angry wondering if they have wasted their time studying for a worthless degree. And there's the questions about finding balance between school, jobs, friends and family, and a "significant other." How do they choose priorities?

I don't always have all the answers. In fact, some questions I can't answer at all. But I listen to them. I offer them some compassion, use myself and my experiences as examples of how to keep going while you search for answers. And, always, how you need to look within yourself to find the voice of God that quietly whispers what to do.

These young people seek motivators that can speak with their hearts, and merely show off their own financial success. They need genuine motivators that are not dressed in a three-piece suit but rather in jeans and a baseball cap, talking to them and not down to them.

* * * * *

Whether it's the women in my audience or young adults, I realize my limitations and that I may not always succeed in helping them. But I try. I attempt to use my experiences to assist them with inspiration and hope. I help them understand that one way to face their future is with a continuing, new or renewed faith in themselves and in the Almighty. I remind them that faith can take broken people and make them unbroken to glorify His name.

1 Thessalonians 5:16-18 KJV, "Rejoice evermore. Pray without ceasing. In Everything give thanks: for this is the will of God in Christ Jesus concerning you."

CHAPTER 17

GOD'S PROMISES ARE REVEALED

S everal copies of "A Light Above And Beyond, A True Story of Strength, Courage, And Unwavering Faith" in my hands, a contract to print them, and an announcement, "Coming Soon," posted on my social media. But I wasn't certain when "soon" was.

"Xiomara your book isn't ready to go out yet. There is still much more for you to learn and these need to be written into this book." Those are the words I heard in my mind. God gently reminded me that there were upcoming events that were important.

I presented Florida International University with the idea for programs built around CHIME. My hope was that we could work together to develop the programs. I knew that there was need for the South Florida community. Unfortunately, I was politely thanked for my interest and sent on my way.

I continued working on my own and was able to attend, "My alma mater, Florida International University, inauguration of the Young Adults program that I had worked so hard to develop over the past years; but without any, any credit to me for the initial idea? But I trusted in God that my knowing what I had done was reward enough and, as we know, "pride goeth before a fall." So, in November 2016, the "FIU Young Alumni Council," was being integrated as part of "FIU Alumni Chapters & Affinity Councils."

The inauguration was glorious. Though the event was held in a large space, it seemed intimate. The school logo, a Panther, was everywhere; it symbolized the spirit and values of Truth, Freedom, Respect, Responsibility, and Excellence that everyone in the room hoped would be accomplished with this integration. To me the most unforgettable moment was to seeing students and alumni together in the same room, sharing ideas and experiences and empowering each other.

This, I thought, was why I had hesitated in publishing my book. This was what the Almighty suggested I wait for. I would include this in my book and be done. Yet, something still nagged at me. I felt that more had yet to unfold.

In January 2017, I attended the FIU 2017 Women's Alumni Council Planning Workshop and it became apparent to me that God had this in mind. I had already introduced my CHIME for Women title as "A New Face, A New Era," and now FIU revealed the event title "A New Year, A New Me." It called my attention and God guided me to be present to witness His own plans. It was beautiful and reassuring to see the similarities in the event titles and definitely the program's mission. I saw it as part of the stepping-stones that God laid before me to follow along my unknown path. I could work with and through my alma mater to change lives and empower others.

I wondered, *"Is this the big door you had promised me, Lord?"* And I knew in my heart and with so many evidence at hand, that it was. I'm glad that FIU was inspired and developed these amazing programs that will reach thousands of students and alumni for many years to come.

I said a prayer of thanks and heard these words *"Xiomara, I used you as an individual and the University as a larger institution to make my testimony, pronounced and visual, so you can trust me that my handprints were there every step of the way. So you can identify that I have been talking to you all along. That you may find reward in helping others and solace in your so doing."* My heart and mind were calm and at peace. I felt blessed. I was humbled to have been chosen and given this task, but pleased that I had been chosen. And I was grateful to know that I was following His commands by Faith.

I thought about all that I had been through—domestic violence, kidnapping, a horrible accident, heart problems, one failed marriage, a difficult pregnancy, and the death of my beloved mother. To think about them as a list of events in my life made one thing clear and that was echoed in the whisper I heard in what I recognized as God's voice,

"Here is your testimony Xiomara, go and share it. Help others make a positive of the obstacles they have

encountered. Help them understand, as you have understood, that I will guide them if they have faith."

* * * * *

My passion to help others through CHIME and collaborating with FIU will never end. We both work on the same cause but in our own way. We both have as a goal to make our next generation a promising one.

I produced and recorded my CHIME Women's and Young Adult programs from my living room, and it is being used by state organizations. I am honored to be helping others and proud that God has used me throughout this long journey.

CHIME TEACHING AND LEARNING, bringing Change-Hope, Inspiration, Motivation, and Empower to Young Adults.

FLORIDA INTERNATIONAL UNIVERSITY ALUMNI
ASSOCIATION, Young Alumni Council.

Afterword

As I finish this book, I have now been given an answer
as to what happened to my *Papi*. and an answer to my
questions about his final moments.

My father was dying of lung cancer and weak. He
was cared for at the home of a relative. "Cuando vienen
mis muchachitas?" ("When are my little girls coming?")
he would ask. Not knowing when or if anyone was
coming, they would answer "Pronto" (Soon") to keep
him calm and reassure him. He carried the hope of
seeing me with him those final days.

One afternoon when he seemed to take too long in the bathroom, they knocked on the door, "Bertico?" they asked . When there was no reply they open the door to find my father on the floor. He had suffered a heart attack but died on the cold bed of the ambulance on his way to the hospital.

Knowing that he was dying, my father had donated his body to cancer research. It was a selfless act that I am certain he believed help atone for some of the things he had done in his life. And, now know that my *Papi*, the loving, caring father of my childhood memory, passed realizing that he may now do more good than he had done before.

I have always been associated with Florida International University and take great pride in being a "Panther" and alum. My father never received a good education, let alone a university education, yet he did make it to college; in fact, to F.I.U. *As God willed it, my FATHER's remains were delivered to F.I.U. for research.*

I now have the answers to the questions I asked in the preface to this book. It breaks my heart to know these painful answers, but God knew I needed to know; that I needed closure. And, now I have it.

We are, as much as we might deny it, made up of the totality of our life experiences—be they good or bad. With God's help we remember the good and forgive, if not forget, the bad. And so it is that I bid my father, Rest In Peace.

CHAPTER 18

THE GLISTENING SOUL WITHIN

1 Matthew 6:22-23 KJV, "The LIGHT of the body is the eye: therefore thine eye be single, thy whole body shall be full of light. But if thine eye be evil, thy whole body shall be full of darkness. If therefore the LIGHT that is in thee be darkness how great is that darkness!"

"I can see the blue sky, I can see the white clouds, I can see the different types of flowers, the greenery, and everything that is in my surroundings. I'm blessed and thankful every day of my life for the privilege of enjoying it all."

But, what happens when you are in the dark? Literally.

Despite all that I had been through, I always found a way to survive, that survival serving as a testimony that God used every single one of my weaknesses as an opportunity to show His strength in my life. Fortitude and blessings, blessings of fortitude. Onward, always onward. God was the light in my darkness—metaphorically speaking. But I truly needed His light when I lost sight in my one eye.

I have always had a love of fashion and design, following the latest trends, learning as much as I could about clothing, accessories, hair and makeup. Yet I was never vain about my appearance. Don't misunderstand, I LOVE to look my best at all times and adore getting glamorous for formal events. That's not vanity, that's smart business.

One thing I learned in Marketing was that you have to keep your product front and center, as appealing as possible, and always show it in a favorable light. As a business woman and an inspirational speaker, my product was my image, my brand was me! So looking my best—whether in a formal gown or the right jeans and tee—simply makes sense. Encouraged by friends to change a little, I decided on a makeover.

I told my husband that I was thinking about cutting my hair. "The new trend is short hair. I think it will refresh my image. Besides, I've worn my hair long for almost twenty years." He could hear in my voice that this was more a declaration than a request for permission.

"You'll look beautiful no matter what," he said.

Haircuts, new colors for eye shadow and lipsticks, new, silky smooth face powders, and some new wardrobe were all part of creating "an exciting new me."

"Did you know that you have a ridge in the middle of your eyebrows?" one of my friends told me. I looked in a mirror. She was right.

"It's not really that noticeable…still, if I were you, I'd get Botox."

"Botox?" I asked.

"Sure, why not? You'll see results within a day or two. You should do it!"

I thought about for a moment. Was it too much? Was I becoming too vain? Oh, what the heck! I've got to look my best to do what I need to do to help others and promote my faith. After all, it's a simple procedure. What could go wrong?

"I'm trying to lift the right eyelid, but it keeps falling; and look, my eyebrow is going up to the middle of my forehead," I told my friends. They laughed and I laughed with them. It was probably a normal reaction to the Botox procedure. "Don't worry, you'll look perfect in a day or so," was their consensus.

Soon a week had almost passed and my situation was getting worse. My right eye was not moving at all. Worse, I had lost sight in that eye!

The doctor told me I'd be all right in time and that the estimated time of recovery was three to six months. Three to six months! I didn't have that kind of time. I had business meetings planned, speaking engagements, I had important pending discussions with FIU. Most importantly, my book had to be completed.

"What are you trying to teach me from this God? Talk to me. Is this finally the last chapter?" I whispered as I jumped in my bed, crying like a baby. Not only was I emotional over all of this, but it was painful when I would try to open my eye.

I confessed to the Lord that my patience was running out, and that I just wanted to live my life like everyone else. "I don't want to inspire and motivate anyone. I just want to live a normal life," I said as I covered my head with a pillow and sobbed.

After a few days of feeling sorry for myself, I found my strength and courage in my faith once again. I felt renewed and prepared to face the outside world.

I attended my first scheduled meeting with a little trepidation. I arrived at the offices wearing sunglasses and wondered if I should leave them on or take them off. I was still self-conscious and unsure of what I should do, when the decision was made for me.

"Can you see in those glasses?" my host asked. I blushed a little out of embarrassment, then I removed my sunglasses and I revealed the truth.

"It doesn't matter, "I said, "I can barely see any way!"

Everyone smiled and a few laughed nervously, until they saw me laugh. At that point they all chuckled and then asked what happened, was I okay, and expressed genuine concern for my predicament.

From then on I continued to be honest about my eye and to tell people that it was just one more stepping stone God had put in my path, leading—well, I wasn't sure just where—to a better future. There was a lesson for me to learn from this experience, but I had yet to figure out just what it was.

However, over the next month of meetings I found myself feeling upset and irritated. "Dear God, if you are going to reveal the 'why' in all of this, please do it now!" I could handle the occasional pain and the embarrassment, but I had to know the reason why this was happening.

As time passed I was able to see through a small opening in the eye when I tilted my head back. It wasn't much, but it was something.

Because I only had one good eye, my husband would drive me to my meetings if he was available to do so. I only listened to two radio stations, so I guess my husband had programmed a few of his favorites, because—as driver's privilege—he immediately changed stations as we pulled out of the driveway.

"What are you listening to?" I asked.

"It's a Christian radio station I found a long time ago," he said.

Now, I enjoy gospel music and all music of faith, but I'm always leery of some of the on-air preachers. They usually come on strong and seem to want to hit their listeners over the head with the Good Book than explain the Good News it contains. I was about to reach over and change the channel when I began to cry.

The song that had started touched my soul. *Eye of the Storm* was playing and as I listened, I could feel the hand of the Holy Spirit touch me. I had lived almost all of my life in the eye of the storm; witnessing tragedies all around me, occasionally touching that eye wall and experiencing the pain myself.

"You okay?" my husband asked.

I nodded my head and said, "You know, I really think I am!"

One afternoon I was at a therapy session when the therapist asked me if I minded a little music, other than the background music they always played. She took her radio and turned it on. It was the same radio station my husband listened to.

Midway through my session, she saw me start to cry.

"Did I hurt you?" she asked.

"No," I said. "That song that's playing was one I remember from my mother's funeral."

"Well, then, that's a happy-sad song," she said. "Your mother's at rest, at peace, but I'll bet she's happy she raised a daughter who still loves and misses her so much." She rolled me over and added, "See, she still inspires you."

Inspiration. Yes, that was it! I sat up and asked her to hand me my purse. I reached in and pulled out the dog-eared, annotated proof copy of my book.

"See this?" I asked, holding the book out for her to see. "This is the book I'm writing about my life. I wasn't sure if I could finish it, but now I know I can. One-eyed or blind, I see with the light, God's light, that's within me. I'm inspired by God and hope to inspire others by my witness."

"Amen to that!" she said and I put the book back in my purse.

She asked me about the book as we finished my session and I told her a little about my hopes for it. As I related a few details of my life, she stopped for a second. "No way!" she said.

My therapist, this random person in my life, had attended the same little white church I had discovered almost fourteen years ago! We finished the session and talked a little longer, reminiscing about our time there. Before I left, we both knelt down and prayed to praise God for His love, devotion, and understanding.

I continued to work on my book, a memoir to help explain what has made me who I am today, to show that anyone can come through adversity, that all it takes is understanding of the miracles that God had given us and through the strength of belief in a better tomorrow through our faith in God.

I announced that I was finishing my book and gave my personal testimony live on Facebook. I am happy to say that thousands of viewers watched it. There I was, one-eyed, just a little makeup, showing myself as I am and giving witness before my viewers that God's strength delivers us all.

I conclude my broadcast by saying, "I lost sight in one eye, but as I heard God whisper to me, 'Do not stumble blindly through the darkness. Tell them I am the light that comes from above and it is for all to receive and share with the world.'"

I have received thousands of messages thanking me for my witness and saying that I had indeed given them hope. When I read such a message, I cry.

But, as I always say, "There are tears of joy and tears of sadness, and as long as you can tell the difference, then the tears of joy serve to cleanse the soul and open a beautiful channel of communication with God."

Everything happens for a reason and that has always been my life philosophy. We can never know what God had planned for us, so it's best to listen with our heart and proceed as He dictates. Harm no one; love yourself and then you can love others; we are all stumbling through the darkness, so if you can bring a little light to someone else—do so!

After all I've been through I realize that I am the light that shines for Him no matter where I go. I'm the light that can help people find solace and rejoice.

This is my story and I'm proud to say that despite all my losses and struggles, I have been witness to the Light. A light that shines both within me and throughout all existence. A light that is truly, "A Light Above And Beyond.

"I am a child of LIGHT that comes from ABOVE. God put in my heart His LIGHT to shine way BEYOND to Glorify His name every day of my life."

IN CLOSING

We all have a story to tell. We all have a "dark side" in our lives; one that we usually refuse to discuss. I thank you for reading about my life and my "dark sides."

My purpose in writing this is to inspire hope in my readers and to show that acknowledging God is the first step in overcoming the obstacles in life. I know it was in mine.

Learn how to hear His voice. I urge you to pray, to meditate, to find an understanding that will allow you to hear the quiet voice of God and feel His presence in your life.

An answer to a prayer may take days, months, or years. And sometimes we might not even notice that our prayer was answered, because it was answered in some unusual way. But, God's timing is perfect. He knows where, when, and to whom He chooses to deliver a message. He knows what we need when we only seem to know what we want.

Many of us live in a world of despair and unhappiness. It seems unfair and unbalanced. However, there is one simple part of the equation that might be missing; you might be missing God in your life. See the light; be free and happy. Recognize and accept yourself for who you, regardless of what other people think or say. Do not allow fear, or anyone's threats or retaliation stand in your way. Believe, have faith, do good, and use the opportunities that God is giving you every day.

Give God the thanks and praise He deserves. Acknowledge the Almighty's role in your life. Praising God can be as simple as thinking about Him when you are trying to make a decision. A prayerful, "what should I do?"

He may deliver a message to you in many different ways. They may come to you as random thoughts, feelings, and dreams. The thoughts may pass through your mind without an explanation. The feeling may be an inner voice that gives you calm. He may show you signs over and over until we finally recognize them and understand that God has just spoken to you.

It isn't easy, for many times the voice you hear or the feeling that you feel is not Gods. It take discernment to know what is right.

Keep God within you and you can see His wonders without you. However, don't take God for granted. The

Almighty is not a vending machine that you drop a prayer into as payment and a miracle pops out as your purchase.

God's word or voice is not to be confused or used in vain

> 1 Ezekiel 44:23 KJV, "And they shall teach my people the difference between the holy and profane, and cause them to discern between the unclean and the clean."

I once overheard a man talking to a lady that worked in a department store.

"I heard you talking on the phone about going to church next Sunday, "he said. I need to pray, but I don't know how to start. How do you pray? The more I think about it, the more selfish and guilty I feel asking God for anything."

"Excuse me, Sir," I said. "I didn't mean eavesdrop but I overheard what you said; may I give you my opinion?"

The saleslady looked at me and said, "I'm glad you're here because I do not know what exactly to say."

"You entered into a conversation with this lady, right? Do exactly the same with God. There is no difference. He has been listening and waiting patiently to communicate with you," I replied.

His face changed; his eyes started shining and he gave me a gorgeous, broad smile. "Thank you," he said and reached out to shake my hand. I saw hope in his eyes and a lightness of spirit as he walked away.

* * * * *

Revealing your truth to the public is petrifying and it takes a lot of courage. I don't live in despair over it nor am I ashamed of my past. The world is full of people with problems, deficiencies, broken families, and addictions.

"God uses broken people and makes them whole," as it says in Scripture. He uses people, just like me, that have gone through difficulties to glorify His name. In my heart and soul, there is only space for forgiveness, understanding, and righteousness.

My prayer to the Almighty as I finish sharing my life with you, dear reader:

"Father, give me strength and discernment after this book is launched. Allow me to continue to give hope and inspiration. Send your Angels to protect me from those who would chastise me for my witness. Lift me up as you have always done when I falter and fall. Close my eyes and ears so no negative judgments can

divert me from listening to your voice and will. Touch the souls of those you already know are intended to serve you, for the righteous cause you have already started. And, heal those souls that receive my message as a promise of your love, ~Amen."

In closing, this book is not about a single church, denomination, or religion. It is about FAITH. It is a simple story of a little girl that lived an unusual life and discovered hope. It is about a little girl that lived in the dark but searched for a light through faith. Who, during her suffering, abuse, and despair, humbled herself under God's mighty hands and felt Him lift her up. And now, as a woman, continues serving her Lord.

As long as He is with me, I will always have STRENGTH, COURAGE, and UNWAVERING FAITH.

STRENGTH:

1 Psalm 27:1 KJV, "The LORD is my light and salvation; whom shall fear? The LORD is the strength."

COURAGE:

1 Psalm 31:24 KJV, "Be strong and let your heart take courage all you who hope in the Lord."

UNWAVERING FAITH:

1 John 12:36-37 KJV, "While ye have light, believe in the light, that ye may be the children of light. These things spake Jesus and departed, and did hide himself from the. 37 But though he had done so many miracles before them, yet they believed not on him."

1 James 1:17 KJV, "Every good gift and every perfect gift is from above, and cometh down from the Father of Lights, with whom is no variableness, neither shadow of turning."

My mother did not take me away from my father's sight, rather I believe that I took her away from his. One story might have finished, but another has just begun.

R.I.P.
"MIMI AND PAPI"
1945-2013 & 1936-2012

"A TROUBLED LOVE IN THIS WORLD, MAY BLOSSOM INTO A BEAUTIFUL ONE IN HEAVEN"

ACKNOWLEDGEMENTS

To my family, as small as it is, but more united than many larger ones. Everything that we have gone through together, is priceless. We have all lived difficult and beautiful times. We have conquered and developed a family with great values-always having in our minds and hearts the gift that God gave us-be humble and give without expecting anything in return. We have touched and helped so many that we knew needed help and others which we knew not if they needed. But, with God by our side, we still did it with love, following God's will—"Help others."

Our love, respect, caring, and endless support is what keeps us together; my SISTER, Merida; my brother-in-law, who to me is my brother, Jose; my nephew and niece whom I adore, Bryan and Valery. You both came into my life and gave me hope and happiness since the minute I stared into your eyes. And now, that you are adults, you are both a vivid testimony and the perfect example to others, of how good values can be taught. I couldn't be more proud, and may God always use you to serve him. To my mother who devoted her time and limited herself from her own lifestyle through the first trimester of my pregnancy. She took me in her arms and sheltered me in her house due to my high risk pregnancy. Sleeping on a sofa so I can sleep on her bed to being unable to cook her favorite meals because I could not withstand smells were among her sacrifices. She loved Kassandra since the day she was conceived. They bonded in such a way that they slept together till her last days. *THANK YOU.*

To my Husband, Felix, for being with me in good times and bad, with devotion and unconditional love. For allowing me and listening to my needs and desires to make my dreams come true. For recording my decorating segments and my individual messages to my fans; in a small room at home. For believing me when I said I was going to record a TV Show. For watching over me as I was writing magazine and newspaper articles. And, definitively, for the current support in this new adventure of CHIME Network, which he continues to record; still in that small room at home. *THANK YOU.*

To my Daughter, for encouraging me on a daily basis; from enjoying going with me house hunting for my property investments, to writing this book. She was my biggest fan throughout the entire process of my TV Show exposure, and the writing of magazine and newspaper columns. It gives me pleasure that as I'm going on new journeys, she is always watching me from behind the scenes. These qualities are well expressed with her excellent behavior, as she demonstrates the desire to learn new things every day. But, as I keep saying, encouraging me in the process of this book is, indeed what I needed the most and that is just what she did. Although she knows that she can't read this book, when she found out that this story is about a little girl, she used her imagination, her love for reading, and writing skills, and created the first sentences of, "A Light Above and Beyond." *THANK YOU, mi amor.*

To my Team from *El Show de Xiomara Martinez:* Manuel Nivar for his kindness through the first stage of the show; Arturo Lorde and Oriol Vatelia, co-producers of the show, for believing in me every time I said, "Let's make this TV coverage without a script or location," and still followed me. For all the fun times we spent, recording and creating the intro of the show until the end of the last show. For the late hours, we spent at night editing. For sharing with me a simple bottle of water, to a surprise cake they brought me the day of my birthday at 4 a.m. while editing one of the shows. These are priceless moments that God has given me and they will always stay in my heart and mind. *THANK YOU.*

To my makeup and hair designer, Yaneth Gray, who became more than a friend. Her kindness and understanding heart through difficult times is incredibly appreciated and irreplaceable. She helped in my professional image behind *El Xiomara Martinez* with her incredible hands and talent, but most importantly she helped me enhance my personal image. *THANK YOU.*

To my Photographers, Levis Aguila and Hector Gomez from Lights On Photography, for capturing every single image not only behind, *Xiomara Martinez, "El Show de Xiomara Martinez,"* but for this book. For the late night photo shoots, and their support even on weekends. Your pictures are imprinted in all my social media, coverages, events, and magazines; but most importantly the coverage of my personal and family events. I have no words to express how grateful I'm for the amazing work and friendship we have developed throughout the years. A special thank you to Levis Aguila for the design on the front and back covers of, "A Light Above and Beyond," and for the layout of all images within this book. *THANK YOU.*

To my Book Format Designer, Eli Blyden from www.EliTheBookGuy.com, one day I came across a company that highly recommended you. Since the minute I placed that first business phone call, I knew that my book was in the right hands. Customer service is known to be the success of a business and definitely, that is what you provided me with. I cannot be more pleased with your work, creativity, and professionalism. May God lead your way and I wish you success in your company. THANK YOU.

To Miriam Mendez, my Book Consultant, your talent, wisdom, advice, and inspiration allowed me to continue walking on the right path throughout this journey. You came to my life at the right time. God sent you with a purpose to reassure me that my book was indeed meant to be. Trusting you without questioning your spiritual thoughts was definitely part of "A Light Above And Beyond," book completion. THANK YOU.

To Valerie Williams, from VCreative Concepts, The company that designed all my business, TV shows, and CHIME logos for many years. You took the time to develop professionally and with amazing talent my logos and brought them to life. But, most importantly, your kindness and spiritual soul surpassed my expectations. THANK YOU.

To my dear friend and editor of this book, Debbie Grodman. Our lives crossed each other's path at the right time, with a specific purpose. When the darkness was coming our way, we found each other in the search for shelter without giving up; knowing that we were about to see the light. We have transformed some of our goals into tangible and intangible accomplishments. We have seen some of our dreams made into a reality. This book is just one of the goals and dreams that have indeed come true. Her words and motivation have been one of the keys to the completion of this book. The support she gave me in moments when I burst desperately into tears, as I was facing enfolding memories, are treasured. We have so many values in common which is the main reason God brought us together, our daughters. Teaching them to love, raising them with good values, and using our voice until they can have their own, is our priority in life. *THANK YOU.*

And, special thanks to my fellow author J. Thomas Steele for his insight and contributions.

BIOGRAPHY

Xiomara was born in Cuba and raised in Miami, Florida. A designer, real estate investor, author, TV producer, and dedicated, loving mother, Xiomara first developed an eye for home styling by staging investment properties she already owned. Now, she transforms homes to fit contemporary Florida lifestyles and stages others for resale. Xiomara's work has helped make speedy and profitable sales for her real estate clients, yielding an average of 50 percent return on their investment. Her company *HomeX Decor* has expanded throughout southern Florida.

Her enthusiasm and positive energy allow her to motivate others to cross bridges and build success. She has been featured in numerous newspapers and magazines. Xiomara has also written decorating columns for two weekly newspapers; as well as articles for magazines. She produced a decorating segment as part of the TV show on Azteca America, SW Florida. Her experience, her passion for design, and innovation led her to produce and host twelve TV shows for Telemundo and Univision SW Florida-"*El Show de Xiomara Martinez,*" showcasing

Million Dollar Homes, Unique Locations, Food, and Fun. She has written her first book, *A Light Above and Beyond.*

She continues searching for new opportunities and on her main mission, inspiring women and young adults through her CHIME Network (Change, Hope, Inspire, Motivate, and Empower).

For more information on
CHIME and Xiomara Martinez

Email:
info@homexdecor.com

Social Media:
www.facebook.com/tvshowhomexdecor

www.ingramcontent.com/pod-product-compliance
Lightning Source LLC
Chambersburg PA
CBHW030107070426
42448CB00036B/318